D1596980

Daily Life in Roman Britain

Daily Life in Roman Britain

Lindsay Allason-Jones

Greenwood World Publishing
Oxford / Westport, Connecticut
2008

First published in 2008 by Greenwood World Publishing

1 2 3 4 5 6 7 8 9 10

Greenwood World Publishing
Wilkinson House
Jordan Hill
Oxford OX2 8EJ
An imprint of Greenwood Publishing Group, Inc
www.greenwood.com

Library of Congress Cataloguing-in-Publication Data

Allason-Jones, Lindsay.
Daily life in Roman Britain / Lindsay Allason-Jones.
    p. cm. (The Greenwood Press daily life through history series)
    Includes bibliographical references and index.
    ISBN 978-1-84645-035-8 (alk. paper)
    1. Romans – Great Britain. 2. Great Britain – History – Roman period,
55 BC–449 AD. 3. Great Britain – Social life and customs – To 1066. I. Title.

    DA145.A448 2008
    936.2'04 – dc22

                                                            2008021490

ISBN 978-1-84645-035-8

Designed by Fraser Muggeridge studio
Typeset by TexTech International
Printed and bound by South China Printing Company

Contents

Acknowledgements

I am greatly indebted to the Monday morning volunteers at the Museum of Antiquities at Newcastle University, whose enthusiasm for learning about life in Roman Britain encouraged me to write this book. They were unfailingly helpful in reading drafts, making comments and helping with proofreading and index preparation. My colleague Rob Collins also read the whole volume at draft stage and made many helpful suggestions; any errors which may be found in the text are despite his best efforts and strictly the responsibility of the author. Glyn Goodrick, multimedia officer at the museum, took many of the photographs and I am grateful to the Society of Antiquaries of Newcastle upon Tyne for allowing me to use their collection to illustrate this volume.

Preface

The Romans and their empire have long been popular topics for academic research. A high proportion of the evidence-based publications resulting from these studies, however, have concentrated on life in Rome, on studies of empire-wide military history or on the surviving physical structures – the frontiers, villas, forts, aqueducts, bridges, amphitheatres and theatres – that can still be found throughout the empire and are visited by thousands of people every year. Surprisingly little has been written about what life was like for people living in the provinces, yet in any adult education class, undergraduate seminar or public lecture audience, it is this aspect that interests the enquiring mind.

It is only comparatively recently that archaeologists have become aware of the extent to which life in Rome was different to life in the provinces and that each province had its own social, religious and ethical structures, as well as its own traditions in domestic life, taste in food and personal appearance. Fascinating letters from Egypt have revealed how local laws were amalgamated with Roman law in matters of most concern to individuals, such as marriage, property ownership and inheritance. This is evidence which is denied to those interested in the western provinces, such as Britain, but indicates the Roman government's acknowledgement of the diversity of the peoples under their dominion.

In the case of Roman Britain, we have a remarkable body of evidence from which we can begin to piece together what it might have been like to have lived in Roman Britain. This evidence is building every year and has lately been added to by the discovery of writing tablets and lead curse tablets and by the advances in technology that have allowed scholars to interpret this information. Much of this new evidence reveals tiny details of individual men and women's daily lives, what was on their shopping lists, how they interacted with other people, what annoyed them and what worried them.

In any discussion of how people lived, the archaeological evidence can only go so far and anthropological parallels and sociological studies have to be utilised to produce a fuller picture. There are obvious problems with bringing in this sort of evidence, and readers need to be aware that much of what is suggested in this book is an interpretation based on scholars' current level of knowledge. Future discoveries may well prove the author wrong, but that is what is exciting about archaeology – any new find can alter our understanding fundamentally overnight.

The aim of this book is to provide a short introduction to daily life in Roman Britain. It will cover the lives of the entire population of the province: men, women and children; slaves, freed and free people; military and civilian; indigenous peoples and incomers; rich and poor, from the first century BC, when the Romans first started to show an interest in adding the islands of Britain to their empire, until the early fifth century AD, when the formal occupation of Britain by the Romans came to an end. It is hoped that it will answer many of the questions the author has been asked by museum visitors, undergraduates and lecture audiences over the past 30 years. Hopefully, next time they gaze with some perplexity at the stone ruins of Roman Britain, they may have gained some insight into the lives of the people who occupied these places in the early centuries of the last millennium.

Map of Roman Britain

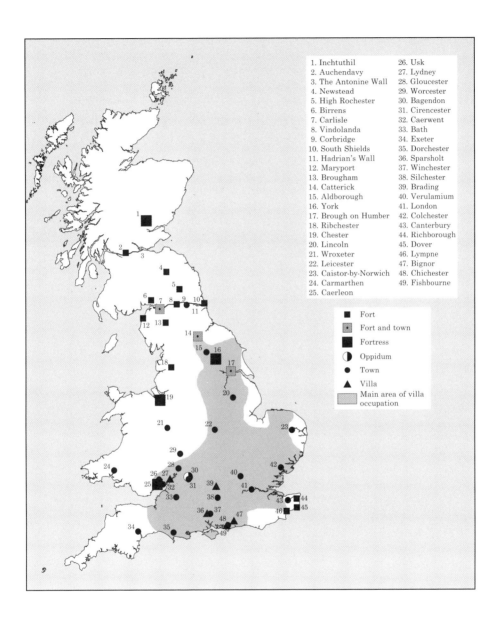

1. Inchtuthil	26. Usk
2. Auchendavy	27. Lydney
3. The Antonine Wall	28. Gloucester
4. Newstead	29. Worcester
5. High Rochester	30. Bagendon
6. Birrens	31. Cirencester
7. Carlisle	32. Caerwent
8. Vindolanda	33. Bath
9. Corbridge	34. Exeter
10. South Shields	35. Dorchester
11. Hadrian's Wall	36. Sparsholt
12. Maryport	37. Winchester
13. Brougham	38. Silchester
14. Catterick	39. Brading
15. Aldborough	40. Verulamium
16. York	41. London
17. Brough on Humber	42. Colchester
18. Ribchester	43. Canterbury
19. Chester	44. Richborough
20. Lincoln	45. Dover
21. Wroxeter	46. Lympne
22. Leicester	47. Bignor
23. Caistor-by-Norwich	48. Chichester
24. Carmarthen	49. Fishbourne
25. Caerleon	

■ Fort
◨ Fort and town
▉ Fortress
◖ Oppidum
● Town
▲ Villa
▨ Main area of villa occupation

Chapter 1
The Romans in Britain

Academic interest in the subject of life in Roman Britain may be said to have started at the end of the sixteenth century, when William Camden pulled together what was then known, or thought to be known, about the topic in his great work *Britannia*. This account was based on first-hand examination of the visible monuments, including Hadrian's Wall, which was then in an area that few dared to visit. Since then, many scholars, antiquarians and interested amateurs have striven to uncover more details of a fascinating period in British history. However, it is only in the last 100 years that excavations, field walking, ground-penetrating radar surveys, advances in artefact and environmental analyses and programmes of aerial photography have truly enhanced our understanding of Britain as a Roman province. Some of this evidence can prove to be contradictory on occasions and invariably emphasise that the story of Roman Britain may not have been the same throughout the land. Nor may life in the province have borne much resemblance to life in Rome or, indeed, any other province. Each new excavation or appraisal has added further evidence or disproved long-held beliefs, and this has led to regular re-evaluations. As a consequence, our understanding of what it would have been like to live in the province of Britannia is constantly changing.

Early antiquarians based their accounts of Roman Britain on the snippets of history that could be gleaned from classical literature. Authors from Julius Caesar in the first century BC to Zosimus in the sixth century AD mentioned Britain in their writings. Some of these works are quite detailed, but on the whole, the Roman literati were not very interested in an island that lay some distance from Rome and the civilised centre of their world. Neither can these publications be regarded as giving an unbiased picture of Britain. Tacitus, for example, wrote an account of his father-in-law's time as Governor of Britannia in a treatise called the *Agricola*'. This was written at second hand, sometime after the events were recorded, and was intended as a eulogy to one man's exploits. None of the literary works was written by a trained anthropologist, and readers may often wonder if the writers had either seen what they were describing or fully understood what they had

observed. However, it is through these works that we know of the
existence of famous figures in British history such as Caratacus,
Togodumnos, Boudicca and Cartimandua and a little about some of their
deeds (Salway 1981). But history is not solely made up of the exploits of
kings, queens and emperors. While political events are happening, people
are carrying on with their lives, providing for their families, maintaining
their homes and working for a living. It is the daily life of these people
that is the subject of this book.

In endeavouring to discover about the lives of the Romano-Britons,
we have an important source of information that is denied to scholars
of earlier periods: the names of real people, which allow us a glimpse
into the lives of individuals. The Iron Age population had been truly
prehistoric, in the sense that they had no written language; with the
Roman invasion, all this changed as the invaders brought with them
not only a written language but a great desire to record their lives and
exploits in a permanent way. In Britain, the monumental inscriptions in
stone – that is, inscriptions, tombstones and religious dedications – which
were found before 1955, were published by R.G. Collingwood and
R.P. Wright in *The Roman Inscriptions of Britain* (1965). References
to such inscriptions in this volume are given as *RIB*, followed by
their given numbers. Subsequent discoveries were published annually
in the *Journal of Roman Studies* until 1970, when this responsibility
was transferred to *Britannia* (journal). These compilations were
made by several authors over the years and are referred to in the
bibliography under those author's names, following the Harvard system.
A consolidated publication of the more recent discoveries is currently
being prepared for the press by R.S.O. Tomlin. Any object with
an inscription on it, classified as *instrumentum domesticum* in the
academic literature, has been included in several volumes of *Roman
Inscriptions of Britain II* (*RIB* II), complied by various authors.

Curse tablets provide a written source that offers us a unique insight
into the lives of people at the lower end of society, those whose names
and lives rarely appear on the more expensive monumental inscriptions.
The tablets are small sheets of lead on which was scratched a message
asking for help from the gods, often demanding divine action to recover
stolen property and punish the perpetrator of the crime. They could also
be used to ensure good luck or to bring down bad luck on an enemy;
a fine example of the latter is the tablet from Clothall in which 'Tacita,
accursed, is labelled old like putrid gore' (*RIB* 221). The two largest

groups of curse tablets have been found at Bath and Uley (see Tomlin
1988 and Woodward and Leach 1993); individual finds are published
as they are found in the annual 'Roman Britain in …' section of
Britannia.

The building inscriptions provide us with the names of some forts,
fortresses and towns, as well as many military units and personnel
who served in the province. The altars and tombstones provide us with
an insight into the families, status and religious beliefs of individuals.
However, such inscriptions, no matter how fascinating, can give a slightly
distorted picture of life in Roman Britain. It is important to remember
that only a very small proportion of the inscriptions of this type have
survived, many having been broken up by later generations to provide
hardcore for roads or structural foundations or cut into blocks to
be reused as building stones or gateposts. There tends to be a bias
towards the military regions of the province, particularly in regard
to building inscriptions, as epigraphy was largely a military trait.
Erecting a large stone inscription was also a financial commitment,
so there is a further bias towards the wealthier members of society. That
said, a good cross section of men, women and children is represented
by the inscriptional evidence from Roman Britain, and this can help
us discover how people lived.

There is further written evidence which provides us with the place
names of many sites occupied in Britain during the Roman period. In the
early fifth century, a document was produced called *Notitia Dignitatum
et Administrationum, tam civilium quam militarium, in partibus Orientis
et Occidentis*, simply referred to as the *Notitia Dignitatum*. This listed
the whereabouts of all the imperial officials, whether military or civilian,
throughout the Roman world and, in doing so, recorded the names of the
forts and towns where these people were based. Several itineraries have
also survived; in Britain, the most useful of these road lists have proved to
be the *Tabula Peutingeriana* and the *Itinerarium Provinciarum Antonini
Augusti* (the *Antonine Itinerary*), which were probably compiled in the
third century AD. In the eighth century, a further geographical list was
prepared by a cleric at Ravenna. Although the *Ravenna Cosmography*
was written after Britain had ceased to be part of the Roman Empire,
it appears to draw on earlier sources and is an indispensable guide to the
place names of the province. All this evidence has been drawn together
by A.L.F. Rivet and Colin Smith in *The Place-Names of Roman Britain*
(1979), and the names suggested by them have been adopted for this

book. Except in the cases where a site is more familiarly known by its Roman name, such as Vindolanda or Verulamium, the modern place name is given.

Invasion

Britain was not entirely unknown to the rest of the ancient world before Julius Caesar led the first Roman invasion force to its shores in 55 BC. There had been connections between the people of Britain and their neighbours in Germany and Gaul for several centuries before this through migrations and trade. There may also have been political links: Julius Caesar recorded that 'the most powerful man in Gaul', Diviciacus, had also been 'powerful in Britain' (*De Bello Gallico* II.4). Several Britons are known to have seen military service in the Gallic armies, and a group of Gallic noblemen were familiar enough with the tribal chieftains of Kent and Sussex to seek sanctuary in Britain after their unsuccessful rebellion in 57 BC (Caesar *De Bello Gallico* II.14). Cultural links may have been developing as well. A rich cremation burial at Baldock (Hertfordshire) contained wine amphorae and foreign metalwork, suggesting that its occupant had been someone who had already acquired Roman tastes. These links, however, may have been confined to the south-east of England; further north and west, the connections may have been more tenuous or non-existent.

In the Mediterranean lands, Britain had a reputation for being a fearsome place. There was a strongly-held belief in Rome that Britain was one of the 'Isles of the Blessed' to which one journeyed after death and thus somewhere to be avoided by the living. Sailors and traders spread stories which added to the awesome image of the country: 'not a man returned from the distance without his tales of marvels – furious whirlwinds, unheard of birds, enigmatic shapes half human and half bestial: things seen or things believed in a moment of terror' (Tacitus *Annals* II.24). Merchants and traders, however, did not allow such horrors to get in the way of making a profit, and trade across the English Channel grew steadily from 100 BC. At Hengistbury Head, Dorset, excavations have revealed a major export centre for iron, copper, silver and tin in the first century BC. In return for these goods, the traders of Dorset enjoyed Italian wine, delivered in amphorae, glass drinking vessels and Gallic pottery, apparently exported from the ports of

Amorica on the Brittany coast. This conjecture is supported by Julius Caesar's remark that 'the Veneti have a great number of ships … and regularly sail to and from Britain' (*De Bello Gallico* III.8). Later these same Veneti, according to Strabo, were to 'hinder his [Caesar's] voyage to Britain, as they were using the emporium there' (*Geography* IV.5.1).

By 56 BC, Julius Caesar was looking for new territories to conquer to strengthen his position in Rome. The geographer Strabo listed grain, cattle, gold, silver, iron, hides, slaves and hunting dogs among Britain's assets (*Geography* V.2), and these would have made Britain an attractive prospect. Curiously, he does not mention tin, which had been Britain's most famous export for many centuries and a vital element in making bronze. The harbouring of dissident Gallic noblemen by the south-eastern British tribes also provided a good political reason for invasion, as it was believed that these noblemen were encouraging their British hosts to come to the aid of the Gauls in their struggle against Rome, and in Caesar's opinion, this needed to be nipped in the bud.

Initially, all did not go well. Caesar's first invasion in 55 BC was delayed by events elsewhere and, as a consequence, was a short event that may be seen more as an exploratory mission than a full-blown invasion. Few Britons, other than those in the immediate vicinity of the landing, would have even been aware that the Roman army had visited. In 54 BC, Caesar returned, bringing with him 5 legions and 2,000 cavalrymen aboard 800 ships. This, from the Roman point of view, was much more successful. Despite losing 40 ships to a great storm, the Roman forces captured several hillforts and overran the south-east as far as the river Thames. Before he retired back across the Channel, Caesar had extracted tribute from several tribes and took with him a substantial number of hostages. However, despite his famous saying that, 'I came, I saw, I conquered', Julius Caesar was unable to consolidate his hold on Britain because other events claimed his attention in the short time he had left to him. It is probable that the tribes living outside the area of the invasion were unaware of the significance of the events that had taken place in 54 BC. Several generations were to pass before Roman troops once again set foot on British soil, and this time, it was to have long-term consequences.

In the intervening years, Britain was not entirely forgotten. In AD 7, Tincommius of the *Atrebates* tribe, who did much to maintain contact between Britain and the Roman world, was forced to flee to the protection offered by the Emperor Augustus in Rome, closely followed by Dumnovellaunus (*Res Gestae Divi Augusti* 32). Strabo also mentions that some British tribal leaders 'procured the friendship of Caesar Augustus by sending embassies and playing court to him'. As far as Strabo was concerned, Britain had already become a Roman province, as these leaders were expected to pay heavy duties on the 'ivory chains and necklaces and amber gems, and glass vessels and other petty wares of that sort' that they imported (*Geography* IV.5.3). The discovery of a large amount of Italian and Gallic pottery and containers for wine, olive oil and Spanish *garum* (fish sauce) at an Iron Age site between Puckeridge and Braughing in Hertfordshire may suggest that Strabo had a point, but Britain was largely an unexplored island as far as the Romans were concerned. The Roman trading and political activities up until then had been confined to a small area in the south and east of the country, but important natural resources were believed to lie further inland. It was only a matter of time before a military invasion would follow to bring the whole country under Roman domination.

In AD 40, the Emperor Gaius planned to invade Britain and annexe it to the Roman Empire. However, possibly having heard tales of the horrors of Britain, his army rebelled and he was unable to persuade them to cross the Channel. Claudius also had to deal with a mutiny before he could get his troops to embark, but in AD 43 his legions landed on the south-east coast. For Claudius, this was an important venture; he needed a military victory if he was to have any prestige in Rome and keep his throne. He was able to take advantage of Gaius's planning, which had left everything ready in place, and landed with four legions and a number of auxiliary units, thought to number 40,000 men in all. Suetonius gave a rather disparaging account of the campaign: 'he … crossed the Channel without incident; and was back in Rome six months later. He had fought no battles and suffered no casualties, but reduced a large part of the island to submission' (Suetonius *Lives of the Caesars*). However glorious the invasion was, in reality the Romans were now here to stay, and only over the following thirty years, they slowly but surely tightened their control over Britain.

Population

The Roman politicians, military commanders and writers usually referred to Britain as *Celtic*, a description that has been used ever since. However, it is unlikely that the Britons thought of themselves as being Celtic, although they spoke the Celtic language or variants of it. Julius Caesar believed that the tribes he met in southern Britain had all descended from the *Belgae* of France and Belgium, but as the Roman army moved north and west from their point of entry, they found fewer and fewer people who could be described as having any links to the Belgae.

Roman writers described Iron Age Britain as a tribal society and referred to the tribes by name as their part in historical events evolved (see Figure 1). However, it is likely that we only know the names of some tribes – those considered to be major or troublesome by the Roman authorities. It is possible that there were some less conspicuous tribes whose names have not survived because their activities did not attract enough attention to be recorded. For example, who made up the 'band of Corionototae' slaughtered by Quintus Calpurnius Concessinius, the prefect of cavalry at Corbridge (*RIB* 1142)? The evidence of the Vindolanda writing tablets has indicated that the fort at Corbridge was called *Coria*, rather than *Corstopitum*, as was originally thought by scholars, and it is possible that this name was derived from an earlier tribal name. Were the Corionototae a tribe or sept of a tribe or was this simply a name given to the local inhabitants of the Roman town? If the latter, then it would seem unlikely that a prefect of cavalry could have given such public thanks to 'the god of most efficacious power' for having helped him to slaughter them. There are also the troublesome Maetae to locate, the tribe which Cassius Dio described as living 'close to the wall which divides the island in two'; it is not clear in this description whether it was the Antonine Wall or Hadrian's Wall which is being referred to, although it is likely to have been the latter (*Roman History* LXXV.5). Many tribal names appear in just one source, so it is highly probable that there were others whose names were not recorded or for whom evidence has not yet emerged.

How many people were living in Britain at the time of the invasion, or in the centuries following, has been the subject of much speculation and, without census returns, it is impossible to be accurate. The figure has been variously estimated between 0.5 and 6 million, although it is more likely to have been between 3 and 4 million. Martin Millett, in assessing the population in the early fourth century arrived at a total of 3.6 million, which he broke down into a rural population of 3.3 million, an urban population of 240,000 and a military community of 125,000 (1990, 181–186).

Within these population estimates, it is, unfortunately, impossible to state the proportions of men to women. These may have varied over time

Figure 1 Map of the known tribes of Roman Britain.

and been subject to regional fluctuations, depending upon events. The invasion may have cut a swathe through the native male population, leaving large numbers of unmarried women and widows, while introducing considerable numbers of soldiers. During the Boudiccan revolt, many women joined in the fighting and thousands were killed during the attacks on Verulamium, Colchester and London (Cassius Dio *Roman History* LXII.2.7). Cemetery analysis indicates that the ratios of men to women varied across the country, with more men in the military zones but a more equal ratio among the urban and rural populations.

According to Strabo, 'The men of Britain are taller than the *Celti*, and not so yellow-haired, although their bodies are of looser build.... I myself, in Rome, saw mere lads towering as much as half a foot above the tallest people in the city, although they were bandy legged and presented no fair lines anywhere else in their figure' (*Geography* IV.4.1–4.2). Evidence from the excavated cemeteries suggests that the average height of men was not excessively tall, being 5 feet 6 inches (1.68 metres), although it would appear that this was an inch taller than their Iron Age counterparts. There were, however, regional variations, with the men of Roman York being noticeably taller than most of their colleagues. The Roman writers were further of the opinion that British women were as tall as their menfolk, but this is also contradicted by bone analysis. On the whole, Romano-British women had an average height of 5 feet 2.6 inches (1.59 metres), which suggests a decrease of 3 centimetres from the average height of an Iron Age woman.

Julius Caesar's description of the men of Britain implied that they all looked very similar and included the comment that, 'they wear long hair and shave every part of the body save the head and the upper lip' (*De Bello Gallico* V.14). It is more likely that the physical appearance of the people differed from tribe to tribe, although moustaches do seem to have been popular. Fragments of hair found in graves indicate that the southern tribes had a tendency to have red hair, but the *Silures* who occupied the Welsh Marches were small and swarthy. The influx of peoples from all over the Roman Empire would have introduced a wide range of skin tones and hair colour, and centuries of intermarriage would have made it difficult to assign someone to a geographical area of Britain on looks alone by the fourth century AD.

Immediate impact

The interaction between the new administration and the existing tribes in the years immediately following the invasion would have depended on the attitude of the tribal leaders to the developing situation. Those tribes who had supported the Roman army or who had come to terms with the new regime, such as the *Iceni* and the *Brigantes*, were largely allowed to continue very much as they had been before, until events, such as the death of Prasutagus and the resulting Boudiccan revolt, disrupted the smooth flow of diplomacy. Those tribes, such as the *Silures*, who were hostile to the idea of joining the Roman Empire, soon faced determined military campaigning as their territory was annexed. In the highlands, the tribes were variously in treaty relationships with Rome or were antagonistic. Most were determined to remain independent, and despite the best efforts of successive emperors and governors, the northern part of the mainland of Britain was never fully integrated into the Roman province of Britannia.

After Claudius left its shores, few emperors visited Britain, with the notable exceptions of Hadrian and Septimius Severus, although several usurpers to the throne started their bid for the purple while in the province. In the absence of the emperor, it was the governor who was the final civil, military and judicial authority in the land. Most governors only served a term of three years in any one province; the seven-year period of office of Gnaeus Julius Agricola, father-in-law of Tacitus, was very unusual. It was the governor who was responsible for ensuring that the infrastructure of a province was established and maintained, as well as directing an annual series of military campaigns, so the first holders of the appointment in Britain, Aulus Plautius (AD 43–47) and Publius Ostorius Scapula (AD 47–52), would have been fully occupied overseeing the provision of a road system, the public post (*cursus publicus*) and an effective legal system. The building of roads was essential if the army was to move swiftly across the countryside, overcome resistance and control the population, while the establishment and protection of the *cursus publicus* was required to ensure efficient communications.

To assist him in his duties, a governor had a large staff which he was able to appoint personally, often from among the relatives of his acquaintanceship. Neratius Marcellus, governor of Britain (c. AD 101–103), received a request from Pliny the Younger to appoint his friend Suetonius to a commission as a military tribune, a post which Suetonius did not take up (*Letters* IX.13.15). Although each governor had some similar career-minded young men on his staff, a higher proportion of the people employed were educated slaves or freedmen who acted as secretaries or file clerks and whose responsibility it was to cope with the great amount of paperwork that running a province entailed.

Initially, the governors of Britannia appear to have worked with legally trained members of their staff in the complicated task of reconciling native law with Roman law. There is evidence from Egypt that the Roman government tried to ensure that some native by-laws, particularly those relating to marriage, inheritance and land ownership, continued to have status, while guaranteeing equal legal standing for all citizens throughout the empire. By the late AD 70s in Britain, however, it had become necessary to appoint *juridici*, or law officers, to oversee the administration of justice. Few of these *juridici* are known by name, but there is no reason to suppose that they were not regularly appointed.

The financial business of the province, including the collection of taxes, was the responsibility of the procurator, who was the second most important official in the province after the governor. Agricola, when he was the governor, considered it vital to 'maintain a good working relationship with the procurators', but tensions often arose. The Procurator Gaius Julius Alpinus Classicianus, whose tomb is now in the British Museum, strongly disapproved of Governor Paulinus's handling of the Boudiccan revolt and had enough influence to secure a more diplomatic replacement in AD 61 (Tacitus *Annals* XXXVIII.3; *RIB* 12). In quieter times, a procurator supervised the imperial estates, controlled the mining rights and paid the troops.

Initially, Colchester was selected as the base for both the governor and the procurator, but it was not long before the centre of administration was moved to London, which was to be the capital of the whole province until the country was divided into first two provinces in the late second century and then four provinces in the late third century. During the first century, however, the capital tended to be wherever the governor happened to be, and as he was in overall command of the army, he might be anywhere on the front line.

Status

The population of any Roman province was made up of those who were free, those who were slaves and those who had attained their freedom through manumission. Within the free population, there were gradations of status, with the full Roman citizens having the highest level of rights and privileges. In the early years of Roman Britain, this level of citizenship was only enjoyed by incomers and a few tribal leaders who were given citizenship as a diplomatic gift. As time went on, however, more people would have acquired citizenship through military service or other routes until every free adult was declared a citizen in AD 212. Below the full citizens were those who had Latin rights, which were more limited. Below them again were the *peregrinae* or non-citizens. This status often depended on where a person lived.

To declare that any woman was free under Roman law is somewhat misleading as women were regarded as 'minors' all their lives, subject to the guardianship of their nearest male relative. This guardian was responsible for ensuring that the women under his care married well; he also administered their property and oversaw their behaviour. No woman had the vote and thus had no political status. Theoretically, no woman could be the head of a family, own property, adopt a child or have legal control over her children. However, it is not clear if this was the situation in Britain, and if it was, how it was made to work, given the country had a tradition of female leaders, such as Cartimandua and Boudicca (Tacitus *Histories* III.45, *Agricola* 16, *Annals* XII.36.40, XIV; Cassius Dio *Roman History* LXII.2.7), and women were used to equality with their husbands. Several British women have their tribal identity recorded on their tombstones and were clearly proud of their independent status. It is unlikely that Ved … ic …, a Cornovian tribeswoman at Ilkley (*RIB* 639), or Verecunda Rufilia, a Dobunnian at Templeborough (*RIB* 621), would have given up their rights without a fight; clearly, as far as they and their husbands were concerned, even their marriages had not affected their tribal status. At Bath, Veloriga was listed on a curse tablet as the head of her family, with equal standing to Trinnus, Marcellinus, Morivassus and Riovassus (*Tab. Sul.* 53), and other tablets indicate that, even as late as the fourth century, when the province had been under Roman law for many generations, women in Britain could take part in legal transactions and own property.

A woman under both Roman and Celtic law was able to make a will and inherit property, but she had no right at law to claim her husband's property if he died intestate; a man, on the other hand, automatically took control of his wife's fortune on marriage, and she was unable to will this away. Julia Similina is referred to as the 'wife and heiress' of Titinius Felix, *beneficiarius* of the Twentieth Legion Valeria Victrix at Chester (*RIB* 505), but the rareness of this inscription should not be taken to infer that the situation was in any way unique. Children could inherit from their parents, and Martiola may have become a very eligible heiress on the death of her father, a councillor of quaestorian rank at Old Penrith (*RIB* 933). Equally, parents could inherit from their children; at York, Vitellia Procula was the 'mother and heir in part' to her thirteen year-old daughter (*RIB* 696), while Emilia Theodora inherited from her son Valerius Theodorianus when he died at the age of thirty-five (*RIB* 677).

Legal arrangements were in place to provide for those who were unable to act on their own behalf. At Risingham (*Habitancum*), a tombstone reads '... rulus, very sweet to his parents; the other (relative), when he (the son) had been prevented by ill-health, was substituted [as heir] instead of the son, following the natural succession', suggesting that a child who was in some way unable to look after himself had been provided with a legal guardian in his parents' will (*RIB* 1256). Those people who had no families, or who were living a long way from home, often joined burial clubs to ensure that they were given proper funerary rights; once these duties were carried out, the other members inherited the remainder of the estate. A burial club at Housesteads (*Vercovicium*) seems to have been arranged along the lines of a tontine, as Delfinus is recorded as the sole remaining heir of at least six people, both men and women (*RIB* 1620). Only those who were citizens and capable of attesting were allowed to make a will. This excluded slaves, prisoners, the insane and those who were unable to hear or speak; however, it is known that slaves did join burial clubs.

Strabo's inclusion of slaves among Britain's assets suggests that there was already a profitable export trade in people long before the first century AD. What the Romans introduced to the country was a complex legal framework for slave ownership. Every transaction had to be recorded, and we can get a glimpse of this in a writing tablet of late first or early second century date which was found in London (Tomlin 2003a). This clearly follows a prescribed formula in which first the name of the seller, Albicianus, and then that of the slave, Fortunata, is given; then her origins are recorded: 'by nationality a Diablintian', that is, she came from an area in northern France. Then the details of her purchaser are listed: Vegetus, assistant slave of Montanus, the slave of the August Emperor and sometime assistant slave of Iucundus', finally the purchase price is agreed at 600 *denarii*. These details are followed by set statements which assure her buyer that 'the girl in question is transferred in good health' and 'that she is warranted not to be liable to wander or run away'. With this guarantee, Vegetus would have been able to sue Albicianus in a court of law should Fortunata prove less than

satisfactory. The tablet also reveals the existence of a hierarchy
of slavery in which slaves could, in their turn, own other slaves.

Some slaves could become wealthy and wield considerable power,
particularly if they were imperial slaves, who accompanied the emperor
on provincial visits or administered imperial estates in the emperor's
absence. Those slaves who worked in the homes of the wealthy or were
owned by governors and other high officials may have found their slavery
had limited impact on their daily lives. At the other end of the scale,
slaves who worked in brothels, mines or tanneries would have had short
and very unpleasant lives. The experiences of domestic slaves would also
vary considerably, depending on the character of their owners and their
status within the household. Some slaves were clearly much loved and
given their freedom on the death of their master or mistress; for example,
Victor, the Moorish slave of the cavalryman Numerianus, may have
enjoyed a very close, possibly homosexual, relationship with his master
(*RIB* 1064) (see Illustration 13). Others were at the mercy of their
owner's caprices, and it was perfectly acceptable for a man to have
sex with any of his female slaves, whether he was married or not.

According to Roman law, slaves were not permitted to marry, but
long-term, stable relationships were formed that were obviously
considered to be an equivalent to marriage by the couple involved.
At Bath, for example, the slave Cunitius and his wife Senovara belonged
to Cunomolius and his wife Minervina (*Tab. Sul.* 9). However, these
marriages were no hindrance to either partner being sold or freed, nor
had either the husband or the wife any rights over their children, who
could also be sold or freed at their owner's whim. In Italy, some estate
owners encouraged their female slaves to have children, as this increased
their investment. Three children called Atilianus, Antiatilianus and
Protus, at Chester, may have been *vernae*, that is, children born to
a slave woman (*RIB* 560).

Slaves could gain their freedom through a verbal or written declaration
of their owner or be granted manumission through their owner's will.
A slave could also save money, if they had access to any, or borrow funds
to buy their freedom. A man could free a female slave and live with her
without undergoing a marriage ceremony; this was a relationship known
as concubinage and was subject to legal constraints. Others married
their previous slaves, which may be the story behind the love affair
of Barates and Regina (*RIB* 1065) (see Illustration 1). A freed person
had a legal link with their former owner which was also subject to law,

particularly if the freedman or freedwoman was set up in business
as part of the manumission agreement. Some domestic slaves continued
to carry out the same tasks within the same households even after
gaining their freedom, a situation which appears to have been the fate
of Caecilius Musicus, who continued to serve Aelia Severa, his former
master's widow, after he was freed, and even paid for her coffin
(*RIB* 683).

Families

There was no typical family in Roman Britain. Although the norm,
as indicated on tombstones, was theoretically a man, his wife and
his children (see Illustration 6), in practice people would follow the
traditions of their homelands when it came to marriage. Many diplomas
presented to soldiers on their retirement specified that this only gave
rights to one wife, which reminds us that some troops were recruited
from provinces where polygamy was legal and acceptable. Whether any
tribes in Britain followed this practice is uncertain. Both Diodorus
Siculus and Strabo were of the opinion that British men took their
mothers and wives to their beds, and Julius Caesar was told that 'groups
of ten or twelve men have wives in common and particularly brothers
along with brothers, and fathers with sons, but the children born of the
union are reckoned to belong to the particular house to which the maiden
was first conducted' (*De Bello Gallico* VI.21). That the Empress Julia
Domna could ask the wife of the chieftain Argentocoxus, when she
visited Scotland with her husband at the beginning of the third century,
about 'the free intercourse of her sex with men in Britain' may suggest
that some version of polyandry, or a high level of sexual freedom outside
marriage, was practised by the northern tribes (Cassius Dio *Roman
History* LXXVII.16.5).

The age at which men and women married would have varied,
depending on the ethnic origins of either partner. In Roman law, there
was no minimum age of betrothal for either girls or boys, and in the
wealthier families, children might be betrothed to each other when still
very young in order to protect estates and fortunes. The legal minimum
age for girls to marry was 12, but it appears that in Britain, women
married much later than their Mediterranean counterparts. The youngest
bride recorded in Britain was Claudia Martina, who was 19, but as she

was married to a civil servant, it is not surprising that her family followed Italian practice (*RIB* 21). At Poundbury (Dorset), it has been calculated, from the bone evidence, that only 7.5 percent of the female population had given birth by the time they were 17, the majority waiting until they were in their early twenties.

For those with a Roman background, there was no need for a religious wedding ceremony; all that was required was a legal ritual in which the couple declared in front of witnesses, or in writing, that they intended to live together as man and wife for the purpose of bearing children. By the first century AD, it was common for there to be a signed and witnessed marriage certificate. A religious component of the ceremony was only introduced when Christianity became the approved religion of the empire. There is no evidence as to whether the native population of Britain expected a religious wedding service.

Because a marriage was seen as a civil contract, getting a divorce was not a complicated procedure. In theory, any couple wishing to end their marriage simply had to renounce their commitment in front of witnesses. Under Roman law, however, there were limited grounds for divorce, and a freedwoman was unable to obtain a divorce from her husband if he was her former owner and unwilling. Insanity was not considered grounds for divorce, but in the case of adultery, divorce was obligatory. Whether the law appertaining in Britain before the introduction of Roman law had any limits on divorce is not known. It is, however, clear from the case of Cartimandua, the queen of the *Brigantes*, and her husband, Venutius, that a British woman was able to divorce her husband (Tacitus *Histories* III.45).

The evidence from cemetery analysis and tombstones suggests that most couples in Britain limited the size of their families to two children. Carinus and Romana, at Dorchester (Dorset), were unusual in having three children (*RIB* 188), and where this occurs, it may be because the woman gave birth to twins. A triple foetal burial at Baldock shows that multiple births were known, although, in this case, with tragic results as the mother was buried along with her babies.

Various reasons for the small size of Romano-British families have been put forward, but it seems quite clear that it was largely due to the widespread use of contraception (Allason-Jones 2005a, 30–31). There were plenty of medical texts offering family planning advice to young couples; in particular, the works of the Greek writer Soranus were available throughout the empire and included some effective suggestions.

Unfortunately, there was a limited understanding of the mechanisms of conception by these writers, so while Soranus could recommend the use of alum, olive oil and vinegar – methods which were still being advocated by Marie Stopes in the 1930s – he was also willing to put forward the theory that wearing the dried uterus of a mule around the neck was equally efficacious.

In Rome, abortion was regarded as an acceptable method of birth control, but it is not possible to discover if this was so in Britain or any of the other provinces. Soranus and his fellow medical writers gave as much attention to abortion as they had to contraception, and anyone reading these works would have been well informed as to the available methods. Under Roman law, a foetus was considered to have neither a soul nor any legal individuality; its death in the womb was not, therefore, considered murder. The sale of abortifacients was, however, banned under the poison laws.

Infanticide was another method of controlling the size of a family. In Italy, the exposure of unwanted babies was an everyday occurrence (Plautus *Gasina* prol.41, 79, *Cistellaria* I.3, 17, 31), and as a result, many laws were drafted in regard to the legal status of any child who survived the experience. The classical writers seem to imply that infanticide was less common in the north-western provinces. Tacitus, in regard to the German tribes, pointed out that to them, 'to restrict the number of children, or to kill any of those born after the heir, is considered wicked' (*Germania* 19), while Cassius Dio remarked, with interest, on the practice of the tribes in Scotland to rear all their children (*Roman History* LXXVII.12). Simon Mays has suggested that the number of infant burials found throughout Britain indicates that infanticide was widely practised in the province. However, there are other explanations of the 'marked peak in death at around full-term' that Mays identified, so the extent of the use of infanticide as a family planning technique in Britain is still unclear (Mays 1995; Allason-Jones 2005a, 34–35).

Some babies would have experienced trauma during their birth, and a number of malformations and deformities can be observed among infant skeletons. There is also evidence that some new congenital diseases may have been introduced to Britain during the Roman occupation. Hydrocephalus has been found at Arrington (Cambridgeshire), Poundbury (Dorset) and Norton (South Yorkshire); microcephaly has been identified at York in the Driffield Terrace excavations; spina bifida occulata has been noted at Cirencester and York; and aphyseal aclasia has been observed at Poundbury. The skeletons of several people with dwarfism have been found. The complaints of old age are evident throughout the country. At Cirencester, 80 percent of the adults investigated had signs of osteoarthrosis, and this was particularly noticeable in the female population.

It is not as easy as might be presumed to assess the age at which people died in Roman Britain. Recent advances in forensic pathology have shown that the presumed age at death of many skeletons found during twentieth-century excavations was underestimated. Attempts to calculate the average life expectancy using demographic models have proved equally uncertain. The evidence of the tombstones, however, seems to indicate that there was a general spread of age. Comparisons between Iron Age and Romano-British cemeteries indicate that neonate mortality may have halved during the Roman period, possibly due to the improved birthing techniques introduced by the Greek-trained midwives. These new methods may also have had an effect on the number of women who died in childbirth, as would the practice of limiting the size of their families. During the invasion period, large numbers of young men would have fallen in battle, which would have had an impact on the statistics, but as the province became more settled, the figures may have evened out. Occasional outbreaks of disease would have created dips in life expectancy – Wacher (1974) has suggested that the population of London was severely affected by an outbreak of plague in the third century, and this is unlikely to have been a rare event. There is, however, evidence that a few individuals had remarkably long lives; Claudia Crysis at Lincoln, for example, died at the age of 90 (*RIB* 263), while Julia Secundina was 75 when she died at Caerleon having lost her husband at the great age of 100 (*RIB* 363, 373).

Names

It was possible for people to be accurate about their age as all children had to be registered within thirty days of their birth, to confirm their legitimacy and status. A birth certificate was available if required. The families who followed Roman tradition would name their sons on the ninth day and their daughters on the eighth day after their birth.

Each male citizen was entitled to the *tria nomina* made up of his *praenomen*, *nomen* or *genticulum*, and *cognomen*. The most important part of a person's name was the *nomen*, as this was the family name and indicated their clan origins. In Britain, this name was often taken from the emperor from whom the family had first received citizenship. A man would be distinguished from the other members of his family, however, by his *cognomen*, which was often derived from his appearance or interests. It was possible to acquire an alternative name or further *cognomina* through life if one performed outstanding deeds or showed some marked individuality in other ways. A boy's *praenomen* was his forename and would be chosen from an approved list, of which only about seventeen names were regularly used. This part of his name was not officially recognised until he became a man at the age of 13 or 14. Most women did not have a *praenomen*. They could take their husband's name on marriage, but most did not do so; at Chesters, Aurelia Eglectiane retained her maiden name, although she and her husband, Fabius Honoratus, followed Roman tradition in calling their daughter Fabia Honorata (*RIB* 1482).

People who were born in one of the Celtic provinces invariably had only one name, which was rarely shared with other members of their family. So, at Chesters (*Cilurnum*), a German soldier called Lurio had a sister called Ursa; he married a woman called Julia, and they called their son Canio (*RIB* 1483). At Bath, however, the children of Uricalus took their names, Docilis and Docilina, from his wife Docilosa (*Tab. Sul.* 94). Why they should have followed this unusual path is unclear; there is certainly no presumption that the children were illegitimate. Illegitimacy could lead to legal complications, particularly in the case of inheritance, but it does not appear to have had any social stigma attached to it. Some Celtic names can be translated; for example, Boudicca's name is believed to have meant 'victory', an inauspicious choice as history records. Other names make it difficult to be sure whether the person named was male or female, a difficulty apparently experienced at that time as, at Old Penrith (*Voreda*), Tancorix had to have the statement that she was a woman added to her tombstone (*RIB* 908). Individuals might also attract a nickname. At Corbridge, a small child was recorded as 'Ertola, properly called Vellibia' (*RIB* 1181). Slaves were often given descriptive names, usually in Greek; for example, in the case of Calpurnia Trifosa, one part of her name meant 'delicious' while her *nomen* was taken from the name of her husband and former owner, Gaius Calpurnius Receptus (*RIB* 155). Many slaves on being freed added their former owner's names to their own.

Education

Throughout the western provinces of the Roman Empire, the preferred language was Latin. For many people, however, this was their second language, and it is not always clear to what extent most of the population spoke Latin. Boys wishing to join the army had to be able to speak and write Latin if they were to understand commands or stand any chance of promotion. Traders and merchants and people who interacted daily with Latin-speaking administrators would have had to become fluent very quickly; those who lived in remote rural settlements may have acquired only a few useful words or phrases. Educated people, on the other hand, were expected to be fluent in Greek as well as Latin, and it is likely that their rhetorical training gave them distinctive accents.

Language difficulties may have been a particular problem for those who contracted marriage with someone from another province. The epigraphic evidence makes it clear that there were many such marriages in Britain: Vibia Pacata was an African woman married to a Hungarian centurion at Westerwood (Wright 1964, 178), while Julia Fortunata was the Sardinian wife of the Belgian trader Marcus Verecundius Diogenes at York (*RIB* 687, 678). In the case of the marriage between the British girl Regina and the Palmyrene Barates, Regina's tombstone indicates that although Barates considered Latin to be the approved language for a tombstone, he felt better able to express his grief in his own language. Whether the couple communicated at home in Latin, the Celtic dialect of Regina's tribe, the Catuvellauni, or in Palmyrene, we will never know (*RIB* 1065) (see Illustration 1).

Being able to speak in another language was one skill, being able to read and write in it was an entirely different matter, and there has been much debate as to the level of literacy in Roman Britain. It is possible that a formal education was only available to the upper and middle classes who could afford to pay for their children to attend classes. Agricola, when governor of Britannia, had made it a priority to provide the sons of the leading families with a thorough grounding in the Latin language, rhetoric and literature and expressed an opinion that the Britons were more capable of learning such subjects than the Gauls (Tacitus *Agricola* 21). One famous teacher, Demetrius of Tarsus, is known to have been in Britain, but as his main purpose for visiting seems to have been to take part in the military reconnaissance of the

Western Isles, it is not clear how much he participated in the education of the people of York, where he is known to have stayed for some time (Plutarch *On the Cessation of Oracles* 410A; *RIB* 662, 663). That other teachers were hard at work may be presumed from the number of writing exercises that have been discovered.

It might be presumed from the number of monumental inscriptions that have been found that everyone was able to read. However, it is possible that the importance of these inscriptions was at their point of unveiling, when they marked a particular event, and that they were largely ignored by passers-by henceforth. Certainly, the poor spelling which can be noticed on some inscriptions, particularly on the Hadrianic frontier, seems to indicate that not everyone had a firm grasp of the essentials. Letters, on the other hand, show that many people were literate and were used to communicating with their friends, making lists, requesting favours and providing receipts through the written word. How far this went down the social scale is less easy to evaluate, particularly as the Bath curse tablets imply that the use of scribes was common. It is unlikely that the tile-maker at Binchester (*Vinovium*) who expressed his love of Armea had employed someone else to scratch his words on a tile (*RIB* 2491.146). It is also probable that whoever wrote 'Austalis has been wandering off on his own every day for a fortnight' on a tile at London was as comfortable with writing as the person who wrote obscenities on a wall at Leicester. Their graffiti also carries with it the presumption that they expected other people to be able to read their comments (*RIB* 2491.147).

Most handwriting that has survived from Britain is on a wax tablet, an ink tablet or a lead curse sheet, although there is evidence that papyrus was also used for longer communications. The wax tablets were largely intended as notebooks, with the messages scratched into the wax with the pointed end of a stylus made from metal, bone or wood. The other end of a stylus was spatulate, so it could be used as an eraser, allowing the tablet to be used many times. The ink tablets were more useful for letters and for memoranda that needed to be kept. The largest, and most informative, collection of these tablets has been found at Vindolanda, but individual tablets have been found at Carlisle, Caerleon and Lechlade. The pens that have been found are all of metal with split nibs, although it is possible that reeds and quills were also used. The ink, as described by the Latin writers, was lampblack mixed with gum Arabic (Vitruvius *On Architecture* VII.10.2; Pliny *Naturalis Historia* 35.25, 41–42).

Besides becoming proficient in Latin and developing their literacy skills, the people of Roman Britain also had to become numerate to deal with the new coins that were becoming common tender. There was a further need to understand the weights and measures which were used throughout the empire. Lead or copper-alloy weights were inscribed in Roman pounds and ounces. The Roman pound (*libra*) was 327.45 grams (as opposed to the modern British pound which weighs 454 grams). Twelve ounces made up a pound, although the Roman ounce (*uncial*) was also slightly smaller than the modern measure (27.288 grams as opposed to 28.4 grams). For jewellers, and others who needed to use very fine measurements, the *uncial* could be subdivided, down to the *siliqua,* which was equal to 1/144th of an *uncial*. There has been much speculation as to whether the pre-Roman population of Britain used a system based on the 'Celtic pound', but nothing survives which confirms that there was such a system or, if there was, what the actual weights were.

It was possible to weigh commodities by using a balance, which was a set of scales with beam arms of equal length, or the steelyard, whose beam arms were of unequal length. The balance was hung from a central lug and worked like a modern pair of scales by placing the object to be weighed in one scale pan and balancing weights in the other. An object could also be weighed by positioning a counterweight on the balance's arm, which was marked with incised calibrations. The steelyard was suspended from a point close to one end of its arm and had only one pan; counterweights were moved along the calibrated length of the arm to ascertain weight.

Fewer objects used for the measurement of volume have been found than those indicating weight. At Carvoran (*Magnis*), a large bronze vessel, called a *modius,* has an inscription stating that it held 17.5 *sextarii. Modii* were sometimes used to check the amount of corn being paid as part of a tax known as the *annona,* but it has been suggested that this example was to measure an individual soldier's weekly ration of 2.5 *sextarii* of corn per day.

All these new introductions would have made life very puzzling for the people who had lived in Britain all their lives, and they would have had to adjust themselves and learn new skills very rapidly if they were to cope. Besides learning a new language and how to handle the new coins, weights and measures, people had to understand that Britain was now part of a great empire, whose borders stretched from Iraq in the east and

North Africa in the south. This brought some benefits, as those who could afford it were now able to acquire goods and services from all over the known world and had access to more extensive markets for their products. New people were also arriving in Britain daily from the Mediterranean and the far-flung provinces, bringing with them new ideas, different religions and even more languages. The country was about to become more cosmopolitan than it was ever to be again until the twentieth century.

Chapter 2
Military Life

The proportions of military personnel to civilians in Britain would have
varied through the centuries, depending on the strategy current at the
time. After the first century AD, soldiers would have been in the minority
in the more settled areas in the south, mostly serving in small garrisons
to keep the peace, assist in tax collection or protect the governor and
procurator. In the military zones of northern England and Wales,
considerable numbers of soldiers would always have been evident. It has
been estimated that the Claudian invasion involved 40,000 men in four
legions with accompanying auxiliaries, while the Hadrian's Wall frontier
alone may have had a military strength of over 20,000 at any one time.

When compared with other provinces, Britain certainly appears
to have had a very high proportion of military to civilian throughout
its history. This may have reflected the difficulties inherent in controlling
an island, whose northern part remained unconquered, but was more
likely due to the Roman government's nervousness about its army.
The expansion of Rome's territories in the first century BC had meant
a corresponding expansion of the army and the need for soldiers to
be recruited from the provinces. By the time the army arrived in Britain
under Claudius, most soldiers in the invading legions would have been
recruited in Spain, Gaul or the Germanies, with only a minority from
mainland Italy. Few of these men would have ever visited the city of
Rome, and the ruling emperors and senate were often suspicious as
to where their soldiers' loyalties lay. While the legions and auxiliary units
were fighting wars, they were little threat to the stability of the empire,
but in peacetime, they were difficult to control and the government did
not want large numbers of highly trained fighting men garrisoned in Italy.
It was much better to keep the troops some distance from Rome, and
an island such as Britain had many benefits, not least of which was the
fact that any military leader in the province planning a rebellion against
Rome would have to get his men across the Channel, and this would
take time.

The Roman army was made up of legions and auxiliary units. By the
time of the Claudian invasion of Britain, there were 27 legions, each with
5,000 infantrymen and a small cavalry attachment. The legions were

divided into 10 cohorts of 480 men, subdivided into six centuries of
80 men. The first cohort was a double cohort of 800 men divided into
five larger centuries. The legions were the main force of the Roman army,
the units which conquered new territories and established new provinces,
building forts, roads and bridges as they advanced across country. They
may be seen as a cross between the modern British Army's Royal Marines
and Royal Engineers.

To become a legionary, a man needed to be a Roman citizen; an
auxiliary, on the other hand, could be recruited from anywhere in the
Roman Empire or even from one of the neighbouring territories. Usually,
auxiliaries were not in the forefront of Rome's expansion but were
brought in to support or replace the legions; it was the auxiliary units
that manned Hadrian's Wall after the building work had been completed
by the Second, Sixth and Twentieth legions. Scholars believe that there
were 63 or 64 auxiliary units stationed in Britain by the mid-second
century, the majority on the northern frontier. Auxiliary units could be
cohorts of infantry or *alae* of cavalry, each with either 1,000 (a milliary
unit) or 500 men (a quingenary unit). A cohort could also be mixed
infantry and cavalry, with either 240 or 120 cavalry men to supplement
the infantry. Each cohort of an auxiliary infantry unit was divided into
centuries, as in the legions; the cavalry *alae* were divided into 16 or
24 *turmae*, each commanded by a decurion.

Recruitment

Boys usually joined the Roman army as volunteers between the ages
of 17 and 25. Vegetius, writing in the fourth century AD, warned
commanders to recruit whenever possible from 'the more temperate
climes', stating that 'peoples that are near the sun … are more intelligent
but have less blood and therefore lack steadiness and confidence to fight
at close quarters' whilst 'the peoples from the north, remote from the
sun's heat, are less intelligent, but having a superabundance of blood are
readiest for wars' (*Epitome* 2). He recommended that country boys were
better suited to an army life than those raised in towns and suggested
that, if urban recruits had to be taken on, they should be thoroughly
tested before being trained in the use of weapons. He warned against
recruiting 'fishermen, fowlers, pastrycooks, weavers and all who shall
seem to have dealt in anything pertaining to textile mills'; various law

codes added slaves, innkeepers, brothel workers, bakers, actors, gladiators and charioteers to the list (*Codex Theodosianus* VII.13.8, dated to AD 380). On the other hand, masons, blacksmiths, wainwrights, butchers and stag- and boar-hunters were to be welcomed as they were fit men with skills the army would find useful. In the provinces, boys were also recruited from the civil settlements around forts and fortresses. Most of these boys would be the sons of retired, possibly even still serving, soldiers, but some would have been from local families, looking for more adventure than farming or trading could offer, such as Nectovelius, a Brigantian from Yorkshire who served at Mumrills, Scotland, in the Second Cohort of Thracians (*RIB* 2142).

That Britons started to join the Roman army soon after the conquest is indicated by Tacitus's reference to an *ala Britannica* serving in Italy under Vitellius in AD 69 (Tacitus *Histories* 3.41). There is evidence of at least two British cavalry regiments and 12 or 14 infantry units serving in the Roman army by the second century. Unlike Nectovelius, most British recruits enlisted in one of these units were sent abroad, to serve in provinces such as Moesia, Noricum, Dacia and both Upper and Lower Pannonia, where they were less likely to be tempted into rebellion by local loyalties. Many of these British units distinguished themselves: the *ala I Flavia Augusta Britannica* and the *Cohort I Ulpia Brittonum* being awarded the highest imperial honours. One unit raised from the Cornovii, a British tribe centred on Wroxeter, is known to have been stationed at Newcastle upon Tyne (*Pons Aelius*), but this was late in the history of the province and, by then, even a unit with the name of a British *civitas* may well have had a high proportion of children born *ex castris* and thus likely to be loyal to Rome rather than having any marked tribal allegiance.

Across the empire, the practice of recruiting men from an auxiliary unit's province of origin seems to have lasted for a single generation before recruits were brought in from other sources. British units, however, carried on with the practice until at least c. AD 130, as the Briton Ivonercas, son of Molacus, serving in the *Cohort I Ulpia Brittonum*, is stated on his retirement diploma in the mid-150s as a Briton, even though his unit had been serving in Dacia for many years.

In the third century, several units, referred to as *numeri*, were sent to Britain from all over the Roman world. The term is used in a variety of ways from the early second century, but in relation to Britain it seems to have referred to military units raised from tribal groups, such as the *numerus equitum Sarmatarum* from southern Russia (*RIB* 583, 587, 594, 595) and commanded by their own leaders, for example the *numerus Hnaudifridi* or Notfried's unit which served at Housesteads (*RIB* 1576; Southern 1989). Men in *numeri* often included more mature recruits than was usual in a legion or more conventional auxiliary unit, and their length of service would vary depending on the contract between their tribe and the commissioning Roman government. These units may not have favoured local recruitment but preferred to rely on new blood coming from home.

The regulation height for an army recruit was theoretically 5 feet 10 inches (1.78 metres) but was reduced to 5 feet 8 inches (1.73 metres) when the army was struggling to recruit in the late fourth century AD. Many auxiliaries would have come from regions where men were normally shorter, and Vegetius, taking the pragmatic view, suggested that, 'if necessity demands, it is right to take account not so much of stature as of strength' (*Epitome* 5). He was of the opinion that a new recruit should have 'alert eyes, straight neck, broad chest, muscular shoulders, strong arms, long fingers' and a slimness of build. It was not always thought necessary that recruits should have all their fingers; in the fourth century, a practice developed whereby boys not wishing to join the army cut off a finger to render themselves ineligible, but this stratagem was noted, and it was decreed that anyone mutilating themselves to avoid military service should 'be branded with a mark and ... forced to perform military service as a labourer' (*Codex Theodosianus* VII.13.10).

Once a potential recruit had fulfilled all the criteria of age, height, previous occupation and nationality and provided a letter of introduction from someone with military connections, he had to undergo a medical to ensure that he was fit enough to survive initial training. Particular attention was paid to a recruit's eyesight and muscle tone, but, curiously, none was paid to the state of his teeth. Having passed his medical, he would then make his oath of allegiance to the emperor, which he and his colleagues would renew once a year, receive three gold coins (the *viaticum*) and, in the later periods, be tattooed. Where and with what symbol a soldier was tattooed has been debated; presumably, it was somewhere that could be revealed easily if a man needed to prove that he was in the army. Some legal sources record that the tattoo was on the upper arm (*Codex Theodosianus* 9.40.2), but the sixth-century doctor Aetius stated that a soldier was tattooed on the hand (*Corpus Medicorum Graecorum* 8.12; see Jones 1987). Wherever it was, the level of hygiene and the ingredients used meant that some men did not survive the process.

On joining his unit, a new recruit would be registered, with his full name, age and any distinguishing features carefully noted. Once entered on the rolls, a soldier was allowed to make a will. He was also expected to hand over any money he might have with him to the standard bearer of his unit or to his centurion for safe keeping.

Training

Vegetius laid out a very precise programme that a recruit would need to go through before he could be considered a true Roman soldier. As in a modern army, the first skill to learn was that of marching. It was essential that a soldier learned to march in step as this was not just a skill required for formal parades but an important element in military manoeuvres and battle strategy. The military step required a soldier to cover 20 miles (32.19 kilometres) in five hours at a steady pace; the full step demanded that 24 miles (38.62 kilometres) be covered in the same time. Recruits also had to develop their running and jumping skills, so that they would be more effective when charging the enemy and chasing fugitives. Vegetius's comment that 'in the actual conflict and clash of arms the soldier coming on by a running jump makes the adversary's eyes flinch, frightens his mind and plants a blow before the other can properly prepare himself for evasive or offensive action' indicates an awareness of psychological warfare, as well as the need for a very fit fighting force (*Epitome* 9).

In the summer months, recruits were taught to swim. In Rome, new soldiers were trained in the Campus Martius, which was conveniently close to the river Tiber, so they could jump in the river 'and lose their fatigue from running in the exercise of swimming' (*Epitome* 10). In Britain, not all forts were situated by rivers deep enough for bathing, so it is not clear if all soldiers were able to swim, but Vegetius was keen that a soldier should learn, not only so he would be able to flee from or chase an enemy across any river, whether there was a bridge or not, but also in case he was overwhelmed by floods. Cavalrymen were not exempt from learning to swim, nor were their horses and grooms.

Weapons training started with shields of woven willow and wooden swords, an example of which has been found at Carlisle. Both the sword and the shield were twice the weight of the usual weapons, so that a recruit could build up his strength. Practice with these weapons was carried out against a 6-foot wooden post, planted in the ground, and a good technique had to be perfected before recruits were allowed to fight each other. The post also provided a target at which to practice throwing the *pilum*, the large spear carried by legionaries, and for archery practice. Soldiers were further instructed in the use of the sling and the throwing of lead-weighted darts (*plumbata*).

Even if a recruit was intended to serve in an infantry unit, he was expected to be able to mount a horse in armour and with his full complement of weapons. To this end, wooden horses were provided and men practised vaulting on to them, first unarmed and then armed, from both sides. Finally, a recruit had to learn to carry a pack of up to 60 pounds (27.22 kilograms) on a route march at the military step and how to build a temporary camp. The practical training was accompanied by theoretical instruction on battle formations. Any recruit not coming up to scratch in his training was likely to be put on short rations of barley, instead of wheat, until he improved his skills.

Roles within the army

Once he had gone through his basic training, a soldier would be allocated a role within the ranks. Most would start as ordinary soldiers and be expected to carry out any task given to them; others, who already had special skills or who showed a particular aptitude, became *immunes*, that is, soldiers who were exempt from the more mundane duties, such as standing guard, because they had particular roles to play. This was considered to be a privilege and soldiers could have their exemption removed as a punishment. Among the *immunes* were medical orderlies, farriers, pilots of river boats, glass fitters, metalworkers, musical instrument makers and charcoal burners, as well as the various clerks who looked after stores and the unit's finances (Justinian *Digest* 50.6.7). This latter group included the *beneficiarii* or orderly room staff who took their precedence from the rank of the officer they served, so at Chester, Gaius Julius Marullinus (*RIB* 532), who was a *beneficiarius* of a tribune, would cede to Titinius Felix, who was a *beneficiarius* of the *legatus legionis* (*RIB* 505).

A soldier with a fair level of numeracy and literacy could expect to become a *librarius* or clerk and, indeed, some men were recruited with that in mind. An organisation with as much interest in bureaucracy as the Roman army needed as many clerks as possible to keep up with the paperwork, which invariably required documentation in quadruplicate. The Vindolanda writing tablets offer a clear illustration of the daily amount of office work that was required in the average fort: supplies had to be listed, strength reports compiled, requests for leave considered, pay computed and complaints dealt with.

Below the rank of centurion there was a small group of non-commissioned officers consisting of *signifer*, *optio* and *tesserarius*, who were sometimes referred to as the *principales* or main soldiers of a century, and all would have had their eye on promotion to centurion. *Signifers*, such as Marcus Petronius of the Fourteenth Legion Gemina at Wroxeter (*RIB* 294) and Lucius Duccius Rufinus of the Ninth Legion at York (*RIB* 673), acted as standard bearers on formal occasions or in battle but had the day-to-day duty of looking after the savings of the men in their units. An *optio* was the second in command to a centurion and was expected to take command of the century in his superior's absence, while a *tesserarius*, such as Pudens who had served with the Second Legion Augusta (*RIB* 638), performed the role of an orderly sergeant. There was also a *cornicularius*, such as Lucius Celerinius Vitalis of the Ninth Legion Hispana who was at York in the early second century, who supervised all clerical duties (*RIB* 659) .

Besides the *signifer*, there were other soldiers who carried the standards for a legion or a cohort and these were among the *immunes*. An *aquilifer* carried the eagle; this was considered to be a sacred duty suitable for a man nearing the end of his service and gave him a rank second only to a centurion. An *imaginifer*, such as Gaius Javolenus Saturnalis of the Second Legion Augusta (*RIB* 147), carried a standard with an image of the reigning or deified emperors and was next in rank. Each century would also have a standard; Gaius Valerius, a soldier in the Ninth Legion, carried the standard of the century of Hospes at Lincoln (*RIB* 257).

Promotion

A soldier was expected to be able to read and write in Latin and do basic accounting; without these skills, he was unlikely to be promoted to *optio* or centurion. The centurions were not considered to be of equal rank: the centurion in charge of the First Century of the First Cohort, the *primus pilus*, was the most important, but even within the other cohorts, there were rankings, and Roesius Moderatus at Caerleon, as a *hastatus prior*, still had some way to go in his chosen profession (*RIB* 341). Cavalrymen in a *turma* were led by a decurion, such as Aelius Gemellus of the *ala* II Asturum who erected a tombstone at Chesters in memory of Aventinus who, as a *curator*, had been his second in command (*RIB* 1480).

It was possible for a legionary or an auxiliary to rise from the ranks to centurion or decurion, given ability and a certain amount of good fortune. One such man was Petronius Fortunatus who is known to have served for some time in York. From his funerary monument in Cillium in Africa (*ILS* 2658), we learn that Petronius Fortunatus joined the Roman army in his 20s and started his career as a *librarius* with the First Legion Italica in Lower Moesia. Within four years, he had risen to be a *tesserarius* before being promoted to centurion 'by the vote of his fellow legionaries'. He spent forty-six years as a centurion in thirteen legions, moving from Moesia to Palestine and then to Lower Germany and Pannonia before serving in the Parthian war. He then served in Syria with the Fourth Legion Gallica before heading west to the Lower Rhine and, eventually, to Britain to serve with the Sixth Victrix in York (*Eburacum*). It was while he was in York that his wife gave birth to their son, a boy who was later to die in the Severan campaigns in Scotland. Petronius Fortunatus may have been a man whose rise to centurion had been particularly fast, and he may have been unusually well travelled, even for a centurion, but his career was probably not considered much out of the ordinary at that time, although it was more common for promotion to be based on the recommendation of a senior officer than popular election.

To rise beyond the centurionate, if one had joined a legion as a recruit, was rare and invariably limited to the rank of *praefectus castrorum*. The holders of this rank were third in command of a legion but often the most experienced in military terms. The officer in command of a legion was called the *legatus legionis*. This was often a senator of praetorian status who had been presented with his commission by the emperor himself. The last recorded senator to serve as a *legatus legionis* was Vitulasius Laetinianus, who was in command at Caerleon (*Isca*) in Wales between AD 253 and 258 (*RIB* 334), but at least 10 other legates were recorded during their service in Britain, and many others who served in Britain were known through inscriptions erected when their careers concluded elsewhere in the empire. Below the legate was the *tribunus laticlavius*, either a senator of lower rank or a young man destined to become a senator. They were supported by five tribunes who were of equestrian rank. These officers saw their time in the army as a necessary stage in their political careers and usually held a command for three years before being moved on or into a civil service posting. A notable example from Britain was Tineius Longus, who recorded his success at being promoted to the civil service post of *quaestor* while serving as tribune at Benwell (*RIB* 1329).

Punishments

Only a proportion of soldiers would have been promoted. As in all armies, there would have been some who failed to make the grade and were destined to be foot soldiers all their lives. Those who were unable to keep out of trouble faced a range of punishments. Each centurion carried a vine stick as a symbol of his office and with this he would lash out if a soldier failed to meet with his approval. In the Vindolanda writing tablets, there is a letter from someone complaining of such treatment:

> As befits an honest man, I implore your majesty not to allow me, an innocent man, to have been beaten with rods and, my lord, inasmuch as I was unable to complain to the prefect because he was detained by ill-health I have complained in vain to the *beneficiarius* and the rest of the centurions of his unit. Accordingly I implore your mercifulness not to allow me, a man from overseas and an innocent one, about whose good faith you may inquire, to have been bloodied by rods as if I had committed some crime. (*Tab. Vindol.* 344)

Another letter records someone being 'deported from the province in chains' (*Tab. Vindol.* 659). To ensure soldiers toed the line, there were military police, known as *speculatores*, like Celsus and his colleagues at London (*RIB* 19).

Among the other punishments meted out were having one's pay docked or being demoted. If the situation was serious, a man might be transferred to another unit. The death penalty could also be exacted; this might involve a trial and appeals but might be exacted summarily, as a centurion had the power of life and death over the men under his command. If a whole unit had behaved poorly in battle, it might be disbanded or every tenth man put to death, a practice called *decimation*. This, however, was only enacted *in extremis* and most soldiers escaped with much less horrifying punishments.

Some Vindolanda letters reflect the exasperation that officers often felt at the incompetence of their men. In Letter 316, the correspondent warns his colleague, 'Unless you ask Vocontius to sort out the stone, he will not sort it out', whilst in Letter 643 Florus asks Calavirus if he has an axe he can borrow; if he has, he is to give it to 'the man who will deliver you this tablet', but suggests that he does 'not give it to him except on condition that he straightway places it in the cart'; presumably, the messenger had a reputation for being absent-minded. On the other hand, Letter 628 suggests that some exasperation was felt by centurions at the dilatoriness of their commanders, many of whom, as has already been noted, were not professional soldiers: 'Masclus to Cerialis his king, greetings. Please, my lord, give instructions as to what you want us to have done tomorrow. Are we to return with the standards to [the shrine at ...] the crossroads all together or every other one of us? ... Farewell. My fellow soldiers have no beer. Please order some to be sent out.'

Accommodation

When the army first arrived in Britain, and during their advance northwards, soldiers would have been accommodated in temporary camps, living in leather tents and protected by banks of earth upcast from a surrounding ditch and strengthened by a barrier of wooden *pilae* tied together in groups of three. A temporary or marching camp was laid out with the front part, the *praetentura*, and the rear section, the *retentura*, containing the soldiers' tents and the central section containing the headquarters, officers' quarters, supply tents and hospital tents. It was essential that each marching camp was laid out to a set plan so that soldiers knew exactly where they should pitch their tents and time was not wasted. It was equally important that camp was struck in a similarly routine way so that centuries would be ready to leave in marching order.

Both legionary fortresses, intended to accommodate 5,000–5,500 men, and auxiliary forts, which were planned to house either 500 or 1,000 men, followed the basic plan of a marching camp, as laid down by Polybius and Hygenus in the mid-second century BC and the third

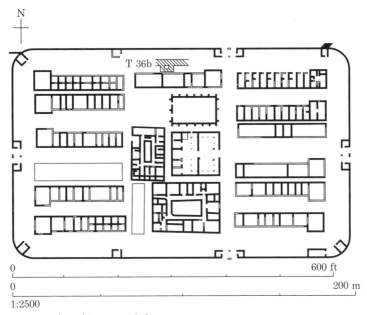

N

T 36b

0   600 ft

0   200 m

1:2500

Figure 2 Plan of Housesteads fort.

century AD, respectively (see Figure 2). The earlier forts and fortresses
in Britain were built with turf and timber ramparts and timber internal
buildings, but by the second century AD, most of these had been either
abandoned or replaced in stone. In the case of the fortresses, the first-
century sites, such as Inchtuthil and Longthorpe, were abandoned and
permanent fortresses built at Caerleon, York and Chester. The layout of
a fort in Britain became standardised so that the central range contained
the headquarters building (*principia*), the Commanding Officer's house
(*praetorium*), the hospital (*valetudinarium*) and the granaries (*horrea*)
with the barrack blocks, workshops and other stores arranged in the
praetentura and the *retentura*. The bathhouse was usually built outside
the fort.

Vegetius urged commanders to site forts where 'sufficient supplies
of firewood, fodder and water' were available (*Epitome* I.22). If it was
a temporary camp in time of war, care also needed to be taken to ensure
a defensible position that did not give the enemy an advantage. For
permanent sites, this latter consideration was of less importance since
a fort was intended as a base from which troops could control the
immediate territory, rather than a place to retreat to when under attack.

Auxiliary forts were often positioned with efficient communications in mind and to protect important river crossings or road junctions.

The headquarters building (*principia*) was where the daily administration of the fort was carried out. Always placed in the middle of the fort, its entrance usually faced the main gate so new arrivals could make their way quickly to report for duty or to deliver messages. The entrance led to a courtyard with rooms arranged down two sides to house the weapon stores. At Housesteads, one room contained 800 iron arrowheads, while at Old Kilpatrick, a cache of slingstones, which had been stored in the *principia*, was used to fill in postholes when the building was restructured. At the rear of the courtyard, there was a cross-hall called a *basilica*, lit by clerestory windows, and with a raised stage or *tribunal* at one end on which the commanding officer would stand to issue his orders for the day. Behind the cross-hall was a range of rooms, whose central one was the *sacellum* or *aedes*, a shrine in which were housed the unit's standards and images of the reigning emperor (Tacitus *Histories* 3.13.2; *Annals* 4.23). At Risingham, Northumberland, the standards and images appear to have been kept on a dais approached by two shallow steps and surrounded by decorated stone panels. On special days, such as the *Rosaliae Signorum*, the standards would be taken out into the courtyard where the unit would be assembled for a festival of thanksgiving.

As the *sacellum* was the most central and therefore most secure part of any fort, it often provided access to an underground strongroom where the garrison's pay and expenses were kept (see Illustration 3). The religious element of the *sacellum* provided an extra layer of security as any theft would be regarded as an act of sacrilege as well as a crime. At High Rochester, the door of the strongroom was a stone slab which slid into position on iron wheels, while at Chesters, the door was of stout oak reinforced by iron studs.

The central shrine was flanked by rooms, one set of which housed the fort's administrative staff: the *cornicularius*, the *actarius* and the *librarius*. These rooms would have been furnished with writing desks and shelves for documents, either rolled papyri or wooden writing tablets on which the fort's activities were recorded. The other suite of rooms was used by the standard bearers who were responsible for the finances of the fort, particularly the soldiers' pay. What appear to be cashiers' counters of stone, with grilles above, have been uncovered at Vindolanda and Housesteads. A soldier was paid three times a year after money had been deducted for his armour, weapons, burial club, the fort's annual dinner to celebrate the Saturnalia, clothing and food – all details for the pay-clerks to calculate and record. Around AD 83, Domitian raised the pay of a legionary to 300 *denarii* per year; this was followed by rises under Septimius Severus and Caracalla, but the precise amounts are unknown. A cavalryman was paid slightly more, 400 *denarii* at the time of Septimius Severus, but an auxiliary was paid substantially less, only 100 *denarii* in the third century.

A soldier might be able to supplement his income by applying for allowances for horse fodder or new boots. Emperors might leave money in their wills to be distributed to the troops or make a special payment or donative to mark the start of their reign. In times of war, soldiers might increase their personal wealth through illicit looting or from the official division of spoils. It is also known that some individuals in peacetime were not above extracting protection money from the local population. Despite these opportunities, some soldiers failed to make ends meet and, through gambling or other extravagances, found themselves in debt and forced to apply for an advance on their salary or borrow from their mess-mates.

Soldiers lived in barrack blocks designed to hold a century in nine or ten rooms (*contubernia*) in an infantry fort; a *turma* was usually housed in eight rooms in a cavalry fort. Most barrack rooms were divided into two sections: one where the men cooked and stored their equipment, and the other providing sleeping accommodation, probably in bunk beds. Recent excavations at Wallsend fort have revealed that in some cavalry barracks, the horses were accommodated in the front room and the men in the back. In most forts, however, a separate building was provided to accommodate the horses although it is likely, given the number of horses even an infantry fort would require, that most horses would be kept in fields or in lines outside the fort and only the officers' horses or those needing medical attention would be in-built stables. On Hadrian's Wall, in the third century, the usual barrack-block plan was replaced by a series of separate buildings resembling chalets in a modern holiday camp. Initially, these were thought to be married quarters, as their erection appeared to coincide with Septimius Severus's edict of AD 197 permitting soldiers to marry, but it is now presumed that this layout reflects a change in the organisation of military units.

The centurion lived in a suite of rooms at one end of the barrack block. These rooms were more spacious than those of the men and more comfortably appointed. Centurions were always allowed to marry, and the evidence from excavations at Housesteads indicates that they had their wives and children living with them. Certainly, the epigraphic evidence from Britain records that many centurions, such as Aurelius Super at York (*RIB* 670), Flavius Verecundus, the Pannonian centurion at Westerwood on the Antonine Wall (*CSIR* I.4, no.86) and Afutianus, son of Bassus at Birrens (*RIB* 2115), had their families with them. Only one decurion's wife in Britain is known by name, Aelia Comindus, wife of Nobilianus, who died aged thirty-two at Carrawburgh, but this absence of evidence is unlikely to reflect an accurate picture (*RIB* 1561).

The commanding officer's house was built along the lines of upper- or middle-class housing in Italy with rooms arranged around a courtyard. Many of these houses had underfloor heating systems (*hypocausts*) and several, such as at Chesters on Hadrian's Wall, were supplied with a private bathsuite. The *praetorium* at Housesteads was a split-level building with a stable block in its south range, probably with servants' accommodation above, a bathsuite in its west wing and a kitchen range to the north. These buildings provided considerably more space than was enjoyed by the ordinary soldiers but would have been plainer in decoration than a comparable house in a town – there was little point in going to the expense and disruption of having a mosaic floor laid if one's tour of duty was only three years. That said, it is noticeable that of all the buildings in a fort, it is usually the commanding officer's house that shows the most reorganisation and rebuilding, as if each incoming commander had his own views on the arrangement of the perfect *praetorium*. The walls were regularly repainted and, no doubt, the family would have brought with it floor coverings and curtains to make their temporary accommodation more homely.

How peaceful the *praetorium* was would depend on its position in relation to the granaries, storerooms and workshops. Each fort was expected to store enough grain to last its garrison for a year and most had a pair of granaries. Each was designed to ensure that the grain was kept dry and away from vermin and insects: the stone floor was raised and ventilators between the buttresses were provided to allow air to ventilate the grain, and in Britain, it was common for the granaries to have stone walls and roofs to keep the contents cool. Despite all these precautions, it is ironic to discover that grain pests were introduced to Britain at this time; no doubt brought in with imported wheat from the Continent (Buckland 1978).

Each fort would have contained a number of workshops where weapons and armour were repaired and where blacksmiths and other *immunes* carried out the trades that kept each fort running efficiently. Not all craftsmen would have worked within the fort; the work of tanners, lime-burners, woodcutters and others on the list compiled in the late second century AD by Tarruntenus Paternus (Justinian *Digest* 50.6.7) invariably demanded both space and a reasonable distance between them and living accommodation, and they would have been sited outside the fort, while the builders, glaziers, pilots and shipwrights had, perforce, to work where they were needed.

One building that was carefully placed so that it was away from the day-to-day din of a functioning camp was the hospital (*valetudinarium*). Each fortress excavated so far has revealed a building which has been identified as a hospital. It is not known if every fort had one, although most have a courtyard building that follows the usual hospital plan. The apparent hospital at Housesteads was placed by the *praetorium*. It had a reception area where incoming cases were assessed before being sent into the operating theatre in the north range or into one of the small wards arranged around the courtyard. Housesteads hospital was provided with a small plunge bath and a latrine, but there was neither an obvious heating system nor a kitchen. It must be presumed that the rooms were heated as required by braziers, but the lack of a food preparation area, given the dietary instructions to be found in most Roman medical literature, is puzzling; possibly a patient's mess-mates were expected to provide a 'meals-on-wheels' service or the cooking was done elsewhere. Few fort doctors are known by name in Britain: Anicius Ingenuus who tended the First Cohort of Tungrians at Housesteads (*RIB* 1618) and Marcus Aurelius (Abroc)omas at Binchester are the exceptions (*RIB* 1028). Two doctors are known at Chester fortress, but it is not clear if they were there to look after the health of the men or were in the private retinue of the prefect. Besides injuries sustained in battles and training, the building of Hadrian's Wall and the Antonine Wall must have been accompanied by many industrial accidents, so the lack of named medical personnel in the province, and any accurate method of calculating their number, is particularly frustrating.

Weapons and armour

On completing his training, a soldier would be provided with his armour and weapons (Bishop and Coulston 2006). These essentials, and any

replacements, he had to pay for, but on retirement or death, they could be
sold back to the army for recycling. Several pieces appear to have been
owned by a number of men through time; a Coolus-type helmet found in
London had four names on its neckguard (see Illustration 4). Legionaries
in the first and second centuries were supplied with segmental armour
(*lorica segmentata*), a short thrusting sword (*gladius*), a dagger (*pugio*),
two spears (*pilae*), a belt to support the sword and dagger sheaths, a
helmet, a curved rectangular shield and a pair of stout boots. Cavalrymen
wore mail (*lorica hamata*) over their tunic and trousers and were
provided with a longer sword, the *spatha*, and a flat oval shield.
Specialised units might be provided with *lorica squamata*, protection
being provided by small metal scales sewn to each other with a backing
of leather or cloth, as well as their preferred weapons. To ensure that he
could identify his own kit, a soldier might scratch his name on it, as
Junius Dubitatis of the century of Julius Magnus did with his shield at
South Shields (*RIB* 2426.1).

According to Vegetius, the legions produced all the weapons and
armour they required in house (II.11), but in the later period, as we learn
from the *Notitia Dignitatum*, state-controlled factories took over.
Evidence from Newcastle upon Tyne and some Hadrian's Wall turrets
proves that smaller items, such as belt fittings and harness pendants,
might be produced by the men, to their own taste, using clay moulds
and recycled copper alloys. While armour and weapons were provided
to a soldier with the obvious aims of protecting his body and giving
him the means to fight, evidence suggests that most soldiers not only
took a pride in keeping their kit in good order but enjoyed individualising
their appearance – the usual image of a legion looking exactly the
same was probably not true and certainly not accurate for the auxiliary
units. The lack of an efficient mordant to use with the madder and
bedstraw, which dyed military tunics the regulation red, would have
meant that few tunics would have retained their colour for long; the
daily muster would have seen a range of colours from the bright red
of the new recruit to the pale pink of the older soldier who washed his
clothing regularly.

Keeping the men fully equipped was a regular problem for the army.
Docilis wrote to his prefect, Augurinus, 'as you ordered, we have
attached below all the names of lancers who were missing lances, either
who did not have fighting lances, or who (did not have) the smaller
subarmales, or who (did not have) regulation swords' (Tomlin 1998).

Daily work

Each day would begin with the troops mustering, the password for the day being issued and a roster list made. Such a list from Vindolanda records that on the 18 May, 'the net number of the First Cohort of Tungrians, of which the commander is Iulius Verecundus, prefect: 752, including six centurions' (*Tab. Vindol.* 154). It goes on to record that 46 soldiers were absent because they were guarding the governor, 337 were 'at the office of Ferox at Coria' and others were off duty because they were ill, of whom 15 were sick, 6 were wounded and 10 were suffering from 'inflammation of the eyes'. In all, only 265, including one centurion, were available for duty.

Most serving soldiers had two meals per day starting with breakfast, which appears to have been porridge or bread and water. The main meal was prepared and eaten in the evening. Archaeological evidence indicates that most soldiers had a good and varied diet of bread, soup, meat, fruit and vegetables. Beef, mutton and pork were eaten in large quantities, with the proportions varying through time, but the meat supply was also supplemented with venison, hare and other game, possibly caught during a soldier's leisure time. Oysters are found in large quantities in forts, but evidence of fish eating by the military in Roman Britain is less obvious. Wine, water and beer were the preferred beverages; milk was considered drinkable only by infants and invalids.

There was no canteen or main kitchen in a Roman fort, each group of men in a barrack room was responsible for their cooking (see Illustration 5). An Egyptian text of AD 360 suggests that each man received a daily ration of 3 pounds (1.36 kilograms) of bread, 2 pounds (0.91 kilograms) of meat, 2 pints (1.14 litres) of wine and 1/8 pint (71.03 millilitres) of olive oil; however, it is likely that there were variations in this handout, depending on the availability of foodstuffs and general preferences of the unit. The discovery of stone querns, for grinding flour, at all the forts along Hadrian's Wall, as well as in most of the excavated milecastles and turrets, may indicate that the soldiers were given grain and expected to produce their own bread. This theory is supported by the evidence of writing tablets found at Carlisle which include lists of the amounts of wheat and barley issued to a cavalry unit for the use of men and horses.

If a recruit joined the army at seventeen and found himself in a *contubernium* with seven others with limited culinary skills, it might encourage him to learn to cook very quickly but would more likely send him out to the *vicus* outside a fort (or a *canabae* outside a fortress) to find someone who could provide a good cooked meal. On the march, each soldier was expected to carry his personal cooking equipment and food supplies and be ready to light a fire and cook a meal on arriving at the night's bivouac.

Part of each day would have been spent in training under the eye of a drill instructor, such as Flavius Blandinus (*RIB* 305). Military manuals of the period recommended that soldiers should have regular weapons drill, fitness classes and manoeuvres in order to stay in peak condition and be ready for action at all times. As with recruits, later training sessions used double-weight armour and weapons. Besides developing their personal fighting skills, soldiers also had to learn to use heavy weapons such as the catapult, which fired iron bolts, or the ballista, which was used to hurl large round stones; confusingly, these terms were reversed in the fourth century. At Netherby (*Castra Exploratorum*), there was a cavalry drill hall in which horses and men could be trained in any weather conditions (*RIB* 978).

From inscriptions, we can confirm that the ordinary soldiers in Britain had a range of ranks and military duties, such as *cornicularius* (*RIB* 1742), *medicus ordinarius* (*RIB* 1618) or *librarius* (*RIB* 1134), and their time was not solely taken up with fighting the locals (*RIB* 1142); indeed, many soldiers serving in Britain may never have engaged the enemy in combat. Those who were not *immunes* would have had to do guard duty, polish the centurion's armour, clean the latrines and carry out all the other unpleasant tasks that were to be found in a fort. On the frontiers, the main activity may have been patrolling the line and supplying the garrisons at the milecastles and turrets. Small units, known as *exploratores*, acted as scouts in the area north of the official frontier and liaised with local people. These scouts usually took the name of the fort at which they were stationed, such as the *exploratores Habitancensis* at Risingham (*RIB* 1235) or the *Numerus Exploratorum Bremeniensium* at High Rochester (*RIB* 1262).

Much time appears to have been taken up with building work. On arriving in Britain, temporary forts were erected to provide protection from enemy attack and as bases for operations. Bridges and roads then needed to be constructed so that the army could move forward. As the army advanced, marching camps were erected. On the northern frontier, building seems to have been almost continual. First, the Stanegate forts were built, then Hadrian's Wall with its ditch, turrets, milecastles, forts and Vallum, before the frontier moved to the Antonine Wall. When it was decided to abandon the Antonine Wall and move back to the Tyne–Solway

line, most elements of Hadrian's Wall were re-commissioned before
being rebuilt under Septimius Severus. In between these major building
programmes, individual sites and buildings were repaired or completely
rebuilt (see, for example, *RIB* 1151, 1234, 1912). The Vindolanda
writing tablets have also revealed that much military time was spent
in bureaucracy: organising and paying for supplies, ensuring discipline
was maintained and checking that soldiers had their leave entitlement
and that their pay was accurately assessed.

Despite the picture given above, a soldier's life was not all hard work.
While there was no concept of a weekend off or annual holidays, leave
was occasionally granted and the evidence from Vindolanda suggests that
there was a form to be filled in with the soldier's name and unit, as well as
the dates and place where leave was to be spent, before the request could
be approved. Soldiers could also anticipate about fifty quiet days a year
which were linked to religious festivals. On these days, there would be
ceremonies in the morning and a good meal and mock battles or sports in
the afternoon. In December, there was also the Saturnalia, when officers
and men reversed their roles and there would be days of feasting and
present giving.

In their spare time, soldiers would go into the *vicus* or civil settlement
where they would find pubs, brothels, cafes and places where they could
gamble. Letter 662 at Vindolanda implies that there was a well-honed
procedure for dealing with soldiers failing to do their job properly
because they had drunk too much, while Letter 656 reminds us of the
gambling scandals familiar in most armies: 'and yet I want it to be clear
to you that I am withdrawing neither from the mess nor from the club
unless … But he saw me, perhaps, at the goldsmiths' or the silversmiths' '.
Vici were not always pleasant places. A tavern building excavated at
Housesteads revealed the murdered bodies of a man and a woman buried
in the floor. This is hardly a whodunnit – only the occupier of the
building could have laid a new floor with two dead bodies incorporated
into it – but the story does serve to remind us that life in Roman Britain
was not always calm, and in the cosmopolitan atmosphere of a *vicus*,
where people from all over the Roman world might be interacting,
emotions would often spill over into violence.

Writing letters asking favours or making recommendations for
promotion and keeping in touch with friends and relatives around the
empire was a regular pastime. Chrauttius' letter to 'his brother and old
mess-mate' Veldeius, 'the groom of the Governor', is a typical example

in which Chrauttius sends greetings to various mutual acquaintances and asks Veldius to remind Virilis, the animal doctor, that he had promised to send Chrauttius a pair of shears (*Tab. Vindol.* 310).

Board games were very popular with soldiers, and few military sites have failed to produce stone gaming boards, dice or counters of glass, pottery or bone. Quite basic items, such as small pebbles, were probably used on a board scratched on the ground whenever two soldiers had a spare moment. Several games which relied on the skilful movement of counters on a board are known, such as *duodecim scripta* which was played on the same principles as backgammon (Austen 1934; Bell 1960). *Terni lapilli* was the Roman version of noughts and crosses played on a square board with nine squares, each with incised diagonals. Boards for this game are known from a number of sites.

The best known of the Roman board games is *ludus latrunculorum*, also known as 'soldiers', which was a battle game requiring great skill. The pieces were used like the rook in chess, and the player's aim was to capture the counters of their opponent by surrounding an opposing piece with two of theirs. *Ludus latrunculorum* was exempt from the ban on gambling because the moves depended on the players' skill and foresight, and it may well have been regarded as a spectator sport as well as a private battle. Dice games were also popular, with most dice made in bone and pottery. Some of the bone dice found at South Shields and Corbridge were loaded, suggesting that cheating was commonplace. As is still the practice today, the numbers on the opposing sides usually add up to seven.

More energetic pursuits would also have been popular. A scrap-metal silver strip, depicting a boxer with his hands raised in front of his body in the traditional defensive pose, which was recently found at Vindolanda (R. Birley, personal communication) suggests that boxing matches were arranged. Horse racing or races between the men would have been organised to entertain the troops with the additional aim of enhancing their skills and fitness. Some soldiers may have hunted to augment their food supply, but hunting was also considered great sport, particularly by the officers.

Dependents

There is now a considerable body of evidence to suggest that ordinary soldiers, as well as the officers, could own slaves. Victor, the Moorish

freedman of a cavalryman of the *ala I Asturum*, for example, was
presumably his groom (*RIB* 1064; see Illustration 13). It may be that only
officers could own female slaves, an infamous example being the servant
of Marcus Cocceius Firmus, a centurion at Auchendavy in Scotland,
whose misdemeanours led to her being condemned to cook for the
convicts at the salt mines. It was while serving her sentence that she was
'captured by pirates of an alien race' and offered for sale; her original
owners' efforts to reclaim her and sue the Roman government for
negligence were recorded in the law codes, the only British case to be
so dignified (Justinian *Digest* 49.15.6).

It is to be presumed that few military slaves were as troublesome, but
there is some question as to where they were housed. It is possible that
they were accommodated in the boarded-out roof spaces of the barrack
blocks or stables, but, in the absence of evidence to the contrary, it is
equally likely that they were accommodated in their own barracks within
the fort or out in the civil settlement beyond the fort gates.

Other dependents of serving soldiers probably lived in the *vici*. Below
the rank of centurion, soldiers were not permitted to marry, but the
number of existing marriages recorded on tombstones, such as that of
Amanda and Julius Julianus of the Second Legion Augusta at Caerleon
(*RIB* 360) and Aurelia Aia and Aurelius Marcus of the Second Cohort
of Dalmatians at Carvoran (*RIB* 1828), as well as in retirement
diplomas, suggests that this law was largely ignored and that Septimius
Severus's edict permitting soldiers 'to live in wedlock with their wives'
was simply regularising an established situation (Herodian *Histories*
3.8.4–3.8.5; Allason-Jones 2005a, 50–51). There had never been any
bar to soldiers enjoying less formal arrangements with local women, and
Robin Birley has interpreted the term *contuberni* in Letter 181 from
Vindolanda as meaning concubine rather than mess-mate.

Wives were not the only dependents of serving soldiers. At Chesters,
Lurio, a German auxiliary, was accompanied by his son, his sister and his
wife Julia (*RIB* 1483), while Secundus of the Second Legion Augusta had
his mother with him at Usk (*RIB* 396). Sisters, brothers, sons, daughters
and even a niece are recorded through the inscriptions on tombstones
and altars. How the army viewed these dependents is not clear. Many
soldiers may have found themselves responsible for the unmarried
women or younger brothers in their family on the death of their father,
and this was a legal responsibility, not to be disregarded lightly. The pay
of a soldier, particularly an auxiliary, was adequate but not excessive,

and the financial burden of looking after these dependents must have meant that many of the women would have had to find work of their own, mending or washing military clothing, providing home cooking or setting themselves up as traders in order to survive.

Retirement

A soldier could always look forward to his retirement. Discharge took place every other year so some men would serve twenty-five years, others twenty-six. There was no prescribed retirement age for centurions or decurions. On retirement, an auxiliary would be presented with a bronze diploma on which his rights and entitlements were inscribed. A diploma dated to AD 103, which was found at Malpas (Cheshire), was issued to Reburrus, a Spaniard of the *ala I Pannoniorum Tampiana*, on the occasion of his retirement. On the diploma, he and other soldiers serving in Britain during the governorship of Lucius Neratius Marcellus, who had served the requisite number of years, were granted 'citizenship for themselves, their children and descendents, and the right of legal marriage with the wives they had when citizenship was granted to them, or if any were unmarried, with those they later marry, but only one each' (Allason-Jones 2005a, 54). Marrying a veteran, would often be a good match for a local girl, as the retired soldier would be reasonably well off, if he had not squandered all his pay and savings on riotous living. There were various perks associated with being married to a veteran, not least of which was that they did not have to pay taxes, and their children would be born as Roman citizens. In the *vici* and towns with military connections, there would have been many families with young children whose fathers were retired soldiers in their 40s and 50s but whose mothers were much younger. A sad example of such a family is recorded on a tombstone in York on which Gaius Aeresius Saenus mourned the loss of his wife, who was in her late 30s, as well as his two children, neither of which survived to their second birthday (*RIB* 685; see Illustration 6).

Some men would have made their way back to their original homelands on retirement, but if a man had joined the army in one province and, after twenty-five years, found himself far from home, it may have seemed more sensible to settle next to the fort where his friends were still garrisoned. Aerial photographs of Housesteads show detached houses surrounded by large gardens which may have been veterans' accommodation, while Ribchester in Lancashire was known as *Bremetennacum Veteranorum*, a name which suggests that some of its surrounding area may have been divided into land settlements for veterans.

Some veterans established themselves within their local community and lived to a good age. At least three veterans are known to have survived into their 80s at Chester, including Cassius Secundus (*RIB* 526). Some, sadly, barely survived their discharge; Crotus, for example, died at Templeborough at the age of 40, but this young age must indicate that he had been invalided out of the army, otherwise he would have enlisted at the tender, and illegal, age of 15 (*RIB* 620). Not all veterans behaved well, however, as was recorded in the events leading to the Boudiccan revolt, and some commanding officers may have regretted the presence of veterans in their *vicus*.

Although the numbers of soldiers in Britain at any one time would have varied, the military, whether serving or retired, must always have been in the minority. However, their effect on the province was considerably greater than mere numbers might imply. Their presence as a controlling force, which was prepared to do the emperor's bidding and ensure that the province was running smoothly and profitably for the benefit of the Roman people, would have permeated into every aspect of people's lives. Their impact on the landscape would have been obvious as the legions advanced north and west, building roads, bridges, forts and frontiers. Quarries for the stone, clay and lime required for such projects would have left scars across the countryside, as would the clay pits for military pottery and tile manufacture. Spoil tips and opencast mines for the extraction of the metal ores needed for tools and weapons would also have wrought changes where there had previously been fields or moors. Whole tracts of woodland would have been felled to supply timber posts, roofing timbers, interior walls and defensive revetments.

The army may also have had an impact on the health of the civilian population. There is evidence that the arrival of large army units in a region raised the population to the level at which it was possible for some diseases to take a permanent hold (Allason-Jones 2005b). The movement of troops may also have had short-term effects on food supplies. The movement of a whole auxiliary unit, with its train of dependents, to a new site would have had an impact on the local population until new supply mechanisms were put in place.

The army's effect on the economy was undeniable. Coins were introduced primarily to pay the troops, and these men, in their turn, required food, clothing and a range of essential and non-essential commodities. Whole communities relied on the army for both protection and income. When a unit withdrew from a fort, the financial repercussions for the inhabitants of the *vicus* and the surrounding villages must have been catastrophic. Individual soldiers may have seen their lives purely in terms of their careers and may have had little interest in the world around them. The rest of the population, however, could not ignore the military presence.

Chapter 3
Town Life

Life in Iron Age Britain was rarely concentrated in large settlements, as the occupants traditionally lived and worked in small units. Those larger conurbations which existed when the Romans arrived, such as Bagendon or Stanwick, were referred to by Caesar and his contemporary writers as *oppida*, a name which was also used to refer to hillforts. The term did not describe the British settlements precisely, as they had few points of comparison with the *oppida* of Gaul or the towns of the Mediterranean with which the Romans were familiar.

The Romans were essentially an urban people. From their origins in the city of Rome, the Romans carried with them, wherever they went, the basic premise that urban life equated to a civilised life, and as the Romans spread their empire, their city roots influenced their thinking. They seem to have had an instinctive need to set up towns and cities wherever they went. This, of course, to them would have been not only the natural thing to do but considered logistically sensible – it is much easier to control a population if it is all in one place; it is also easier to tax the people and introduce them to one's own way of life. As the Roman Empire expanded, cities and towns sprang up; when the Roman army invaded Britain, the introduction of town life was not far behind.

The legalities of towns

Establishing towns required more than merely gathering the population into larger groups. Urbanisation demanded a completely different lifestyle which, in the opinion of the Roman government, had to be learned by example. In the first century AD, model towns, known as *coloniae*, were established at Colchester, Lincoln and Gloucester. These were initially populated by legionary veterans to provide them with accommodation on retirement but were also expected to demonstrate the benefits of urban life to the local populace. This was not always very successful: the low morals and high-handed attitude of the Colchester veterans to the local Trinovantian tribesmen was cited as one of the causes of the Boudiccan revolt, even though by then the veterans had been intermarrying with the local tribeswomen for several years (Tacitus *Annals* XIV). The inhabitants of a *colonia* would have had full Roman citizenship and would have been considered among the Romano-British elite. Such a person was Macrinus, the only knight known by name from Britain, who lived at Colchester (*Camulodunum*) with his wife, Valeria Frontina, and his two freedmen, Florius Cogitatus and Florius Fidelis (*RIB* 202).

Some existing settlements were promoted to another status of town, a *municipium*, by grant. In a *municipium*, the inhabitants would have either full Roman citizenship or the lesser Latin rights, and their local by-laws might retain an element of native law among the Roman civil laws. A town which only had non-citizens among its inhabitants would only qualify for Latin rights, although its magistrates and leading families might have citizenship conferred on them.

Each *municipium* and *colonia* had a council, called an *ordo*, made up of 100 decurions, who were appointed from those members of the male population who were over thirty years of age and fulfilled the land ownership requirements. Such a man was Aurelius Senecio, who served on the *ordo* at Lincoln (*RIB* 250; see Illustration 7). To become a decurion, an entrance fee had to be paid, but further expenses would be incurred during magistracy as the *ordo* was charged with collecting the national and local taxes, and after a decree by Diocletian, the decurions had to make good any deficit out of their own pockets. The *ordo*, through its annually appointed *aediles*, was also responsible for ensuring that its town had an efficient water supply, its drains were kept clear and its rubbish was collected and disposed of. In the later periods, it was the *ordo* that was responsible for ensuring that a town was protected by a surrounding wall. The local population also looked to the decurions to appoint a Master of the Sacred Rites, such as Titus Aurelius Aurelianus at Greetland in Yorkshire (*RIB* 627), whose role was to ensure that the town's religious duties regarding the Cult of the Deified Emperors and other official Roman deities were carried out properly. Even more financially crippling was the expectation that individual decurions would pay for the local entertainments: at Brough-on-Humber, Marcus Ulpius Januarius, *aedile* of Petuaria, would have been regarded as having fulfilled his duties satisfactorily when he paid for a new stage at the town's theatre and dedicated it to the 'honour of the divine house' of the reigning emperor, as well as the deified emperors (*RIB* 707); this must have been an expensive undertaking.

There were also towns called *civitas* capitals, which were establishes when areas became more settled and less in need of military control. Set up by the provincial administration and by mutual agreement with the local tribal leaders, the new self-governing *civitates peregrinae* were based on the old Iron Age tribal territories. Each had a capital whose new title might refer to the old tribal name, for example *Venta Icenorum* at Caistor-by-Norwich acknowledged its origins in the Iceni tribe, while *Isurium Brigantium* at Aldborough retained its links with the Brigantes. The leaders of these *civitates* tended to be from the same ruling elite that had controlled the area in the Iron Age, and the inhabitants of these new towns would, probably, have been unaware of any major changes in their day-to-day lives. Only one decurion of a *civitas* capital is known by name, Flavius Martius, who was a councillor with the rank of *quaestor* in the *civitas* of the Carvetii at Old Penrith (*RIB* 933).

The effect of towns

If we agree that the Romans brought the classical concept of the town or city to Britain, what exactly is it that they introduced? Louis Wirth (1938) defined a city as 'a relatively large, dense and permanent settlement of socially heterogeneous individuals'. By 'socially heterogeneous', he meant that they were largely of one ethnic group rather than one class, which would not have been true of a Roman *colonia* or *municipium* or even a *civitas* capital, given their cosmopolitan mixture of people from all over the empire, although the definition might be apt if one accepts the rather doubtful premise that once Britain had become a province of the Roman Empire everyone in the country became Roman overnight.

Janet Abu-Lughod, in her 1969 study of rural migrants adjusting to life in Cairo, identified two groups of migrant: the first were the bright young men who were looking for gain and adventure and the second were the 'have-nots' who were forced to move to the city because they could no longer survive in the country; in the case of Roman Britain, it is likely that many of the first group joined the Roman army. She also identified a third group, who did not consider themselves to be migrants as they had not moved, but found themselves absorbed as the city grew and engulfed farmsteads or villages in the immediate neighbourhood. She found that the first group assimilated quickly while the second tended to build a replica of the life they had left behind in their new surroundings whenever possible. The third group had already been affected by the proximity of the city, in that they were used to going in and out on a regular basis and having some access to the products and experiences of the city – this is a known mechanism known as the urbanisation of the countryside and has gathered pace in the modern world since the invention of radio and television. This latter group would have been present in Roman Britain in increasing numbers as the new towns and cities expanded. As time went on, even those living at farms and villages in the depth of the country would have had some urban experiences, even if these were limited to using the new roads, paying taxes or visiting the local town to sell their wares. After a few generations, the strangeness of a town would have become less marked.

In Roman Britain, towns had a number of reasons for their creation. Some, as we have seen, were set up as *colonia* to accommodate army veterans and to provide examples of proper living to the locals; some, such as Wall on Watling Street, developed from the *vici* around forts, surviving even when the forts were abandoned; some seem to have developed because of their position at road junctions or river crossings or because of their proximity to the natural resources needed for industry. Braughing appears to have owed its development to its metalworking industry and its prime location at the junction of several important roads, although there is evidence that there was already a settlement there in the Iron Age. Some areas, such as the Nene Valley and the region around Colchester, became established as centres for the production of fine pottery wares, and small towns, such as Mancetter (*Manduessedum*) and Chesterton (*Durobrivae*), developed around the potteries. At Colchester, five members of the Sextus Valerius family were making *mortaria* and stamping their products with their names. In Dorset and the Thames Valley, potteries developed to provide grey ware cooking vessels for the military. There is evidence of a few glass-making centres, such as Caistor-by-Norwich, Mancetter and Wilderspool, which mostly concentrated on making window glass.

The population of some towns would have worked in the extractive industries. A chalk quarry is known to have been worked just outside Canterbury (*Durovernum Cantiacorum*), while stone quarries, whose products supplied the great municipal public-building programmes in the larger towns, were being worked at Bath, Cirencester and Sibson. In the Kimmeridge area of Dorset, seams of shale which had been worked during the Iron Age were now excavated on a large scale to provide the raw materials for table tops, trays and bracelets. The extent of this industry can be imagined from the large quantities of the central discs, which are left after an armlet has been cut on a lathe, which have been found; for example, in 1846, Mr Pennie found four or five bushels during drainage operations (Allason-Jones 2003). Copper mining was carried out in Shropshire and North Wales, and gold mining at Dolaucothi in Carmarthenshire leading to the growth of small towns. Silver and lead mining in the Mendips, Yorkshire and Derbyshire was initially under the control of the military, but during the second century AD, private contractors, such as C. Nipius Ascanius, were allowed to extract and process these metals under licence. Some silver and lead were intended for use within Britain, but there is evidence for silver ingots being exported to the Continent via the port of Clausentum on Southampton Water. Opencast coal mining would have scarred the countryside around the towns of Yorkshire and the Midlands. In the areas rich in natural resources, towns grew up in which day-to-day life was probably similar to life in the nineteenth-century mining or factory towns of Europe and America. In the more rural areas, small market towns, such as Godmanchester and Bourton-on-the-Water, were established to provide an economic focus for the surrounding area.

Most towns, whether they were set up with a specialised industry in mind or not, would have had industrial areas where the noisier or smellier industries, such as stone carving, potting, tile making, smithing or tanning, were carried out. From the amount of industrial debris that has been found on sites, not to mention the abundant evidence of the products made, it is obvious that the population of Roman Britain was fully engaged in manufacturing and trade. Sadly, few craftsmen, and none of the craftswomen, working in the towns of Roman Britain are known by name. Metalworkers, such as Cintusmus at Colchester (*RIB* 194) and Glaucus at Martlesham (*RIB* 213), and stonemasons, such as Sulinus at Bath (*RIB* 105), would hardly have been alone in adding to the noise of a working town while a shoemaker, such as Lucius Aebutius, would have needed slaughterers and tanners contributing unpleasant smells to the urban air if he was to have the raw materials to make his shoes. Chichester (*Noviomagus Reginorum*) clearly had several smiths, as they formed their own guild (*RIB* 91) as early as the reign of Cogidubnus – an indicator of how some native rulers were keen to introduce Roman institutions (see Illustration 8). Pottery and tile kilns have been found on town sites away from the more famous centres of production, as well

as at military installations. On the outskirts of Gloucester, there was
an official tilery, whose products were stamped *R(ei) P(ublicae)
G(levensium)*.

A proportion of the rural population may have been encouraged
by the authorities to move into conurbations. This appears to have varied
in its level of insistence, and there is occasional evidence that it was done
wholesale. It is unlikely, however, that every Briton who moved to a town
did so because of outside pressure. The general drift – as in modern Egypt
or Mexico – appears to have been for individuals to move to towns
of their own volition in search of work, taking their immediate family
with them, sending for them later or marrying when they had had time
to establish themselves. In Roman Britain, we have little evidence as
to how newcomers to a town arrived or arranged themselves once they
were there. The majority would have walked to their new homes; some
may have had lifts with merchants or farmers going to a town's market
or forum. On arrival, they may have made for the streets around the
fort, if the town had a military base and if the newcomer had friends
or relatives in the garrison. Others may have approached the town
cautiously, camping on the outskirts until they had earned enough money
to build, rent or buy a house. Some, such as those who could work metal,
would have had transferable skills; others, whose previous lives had been
solely occupied with subsistence farming, would have had to adapt and
learn new trades, producing commodities or providing services that the
other town dwellers wanted or needed.

A new way of life

In modern societies, the people moving from country to town are already
familiar with money – they may not have much, but they know how
money works, can identify the smaller denominations, have a reasonable
idea of how much commodities should cost (even if they are appalled
at how much more expensive life is in town than they had anticipated)
and can usually count. In the south of Britain, coinage had made its
appearance before the Roman conquest, and although Iron Age coins
may have been intended more to reflect the prestige of the tribal leaders
than to provide a convenient method of exchange, many people in that
area would have been comfortable with the idea of cash, while still living
a basically rural life. In the rest of the country, however, coinage was

either not used or fairly rare; in these regions, it is probable that migrants to the town would have had no money to start with and no clear understanding of its importance or use.

From its invention in 213 BC, until it fell out of use in the third century AD, the basic unit of Roman coinage was the *denarius*, a small silver coin which was used to pay the army and the civil service and in which trade throughout the empire was carried out. Under the Augustan coinage system, there were 25 *denarii* to 1 gold *aureus*. Smaller denominations were made in brass or copper and most town dwellers would have been more familiar with *sestertii* (the largest coins) (see Illustration 9), *dupondii* and *aes*. Dealing with these denominations, either in their daily work or in everyday activities such as shopping, required the population of Britain to become skilled at working out change if they did not wish to be duped or lose their profits.

Roman coins served several functions. Besides their main purpose, which was to pay the army and the civil service, they could inform their users as to who was the reigning emperor, as the bust of the emperor appeared on the obverse of each coin along with a legend giving his titles; these help numismatists to date each coin. The images and legends on the reverses were also used for propaganda, as no opportunity was missed to extol the virtues and triumphs of the emperor and the Roman state to the people of the provinces. A whole series of coins were struck during Claudius's reign to commemorate his conquest of Britain, and *VICT BRIT* became a familiar legend as various military triumphs in Britain were recorded.

Roman coins were mass produced by hammering a circular flan of metal between two dies of iron or bronze into which the design had been incised in negative. This method led to some coins being double struck or one face being missed entirely. Initially, all the coins were made in Rome, but as the empire expanded, it became more sensible to have mints in the provinces. London had its own mint between the AD 280s and 324 or 326, after which most of Britain's new coins came from the Gaulish mints of Trier, Lyons and Arles. Counterfeiters tended to make copies by casting them; these can usually be identified by the mould marks around their edges or by file marks where an attempt has been made to remove the telltale mould scars. Baked clay moulds for this illicit production of coins have been found on a number of sites in Britain, the most curious being a mould found just outside the south gate of Housesteads fort, a position which must have been in danger of daily discovery by the fort authorities.

Coins were also needed to pay taxes. The state expected each citizen to pay what today would be called a poll tax, which required one *solidus* per year to be paid in gold. It has been suggested that some of the bronze coin hoards found in Britain in the third and fourth centuries represent people saving up towards this onerous tax. It also suggests that each town would have had money changers who, for a small fee, would change these savings into gold or, as required, change gold coins into smaller, more useful denominations.

In order to get some money so as to be able to function effectively in a Romano-British town, eat and pay taxes, a newcomer had to get a job. This would have had considerable impact on the individual and on family relationships, unless the family was able to set themselves up as craftworkers or merchants and carry on as a family firm. In an agricultural community where everyone works, there may be gender and age differences in who does what – and these differences may have varied throughout Iron Age Britain from tribe to tribe, as it does throughout the world today – but everyone contributes in his or her traditionally accepted way and has a sense of worth through doing so. If such a family moves into a town and one of them gets work outside the home but the others do not, then stresses and strains develop as the rest of the family have to depend on the breadwinner. Even something as simple as one or more members of the family working outside the house for set hours each day creates tensions if families have been used to working together or in sight of each other all day and every day.

The agricultural rhythm of life is a pattern of major tasks, such as harvesting, alternating with lighter, routine work, such as milking the cows. Communities which are reliant on agriculture work to seasons and the position of the sun in the sky, rather than months and hours, and the length of each working day depends on the season's tasks. A town dweller's life consists of set hours worked each day, despite the season, and this requires a different mindset. In Roman Britain, the migrants would have had to come to grips with the idea of formalised time. Towns, particularly those with highly developed bureaucracies, rely on people being able to make and keep appointments and on personnel arriving and leaving their place of work at prescribed times. Understanding and learning to comply with the concept of formalised time is acknowledged as a hard lesson to learn even today, but it must have been particularly difficult to grasp the Roman sliding scale of hours, whereby the hours were longer in the summer than in the winter. One wonders how anyone ever arrived at work on time.

In a rural community, a family's status is often traditional, deriving from their relationship with the leading figure. In a Roman town, an inhabitant's status would depend on the status of the town – whether a *colonia* or a *municipium*. There would then be the status between Roman citizen and non-citizen to be understood. There must have been many cases where the head of a family would have felt that he had lost status by moving into a town. There is, however, evidence that the Romans understood how important a person's sense of status was – the encouragement of men from the leading families to become decurions or priests of the Cult of the Deified Emperors, for example. But these instances tend to be confined to the old aristocracy, and further down the social scale, the sense of having lost status may have been overwhelming.

The Romans brought with them a new language and anyone wishing to succeed in a town would need to become fluent in Latin very quickly. For Britons who had moved only a few miles, crossed no boundaries or only tribal boundaries, it must have been unsettling to find that they had to learn a new language if they were to work or trade effectively.

Roman Britain was full of inscriptions, and while few of them were essential reading for day-to-day survival, the sense of being excluded, of being bombarded with information one could not understand, must have been frustrating to someone with no tradition of a written language. Today we take for granted the number of inscriptions that have survived from the Roman period and find them useful as primary evidence for the past, even though we realise that they are only a small proportion of those building inscriptions, tombstones and altars. The Roman period is the first in Britain when the names of individuals are known, when the distance from one place to another was written on milestones and when the specific date that something happened was recorded for all to see. This was useful information at the time it was written but only if one could read it and only if the reader wanted to know that information. The concept of having your name and existence recorded after death, and of providing your favourite deity with a reminder of who you were, was accepted quite quickly among the native British; they seem to have had less need to record their building programmes. It may be that the adoption of tombstones and inscribed altars reflected the need for people's personalities to have an outlet in the impersonality of large towns and forts.

Houses

Town living favours nuclear families, and this was particularly so in the Roman period. The architecture of Romano-British towns does not suggest that large extended families lived in the same building, although it is not possible to tell if extended families colonised whole streets or neighbourhoods. What is known is that small rectangular houses replaced the large circular ones with which most rural communities were familiar. Even in those areas of Britain where the rural architecture consisted of large rectangular hall dwellings, the use of the internal space in the town houses would have been different, with the available space being subdivided in a more permanent way into rooms. However, due to the cosmopolitan nature of a Romano-British town, we should not presume that every house was used in the same way just because the architecture is the same. Veterans' diplomas gave the retiring soldiers the right to marry, but often specified that they could have just one wife each; a veteran whose ethnic traditions were based on polygamy would have to consider carefully how the average Romano-British town house would suit a family with more than one wife. Recently arrived rural Britons must have found it disconcerting to find themselves living next to a polygamous family, more so if the Briton came from the far north of the country where there is some evidence that a form of polyandry may have been practised (see page 15).

The earliest town houses tended to be basic rectangular buildings constructed with timber frames and wattle-and-daub walls. In the smaller towns, the domestic buildings reflected the availability of the local building material; some continued to be built entirely in wood while others used flint, chalk, granite, limestone or sandstone. At Great Chesterford, all but two of the houses which have been investigated were of timber with gravel or beaten earth floors. These houses had plaster-covered wattle-and-daub walls and thatched roofs; elsewhere roofs could be tiled or covered in wooden shingles or stone slabs. In the second century AD, masonry walls and foundations began to be used more often in private houses in the larger towns, and this allowed more complex dwellings to be constructed. Some occupants extended their corridor house, with its single range of rooms flanked by one or two passages, into an L-shaped, three-winged plan or a full courtyard plan. At Aldborough (*Isurium Brigantum*), a house with at least two wings had an internal colonnaded courtyard, hypocaust heating system and a number of impressive mosaics, and clearly represented to its owner the epitome of elegant living. Romano-British urban architecture, however, does not appear to have followed a clear chronological development from strip house to courtyard house but was a mixture of all forms at one and the same time. Many houses underwent a series of alterations as the fortunes of their occupants waxed and waned, and it was not uncommon for a house to expand to incorporate its neighbours. At Canterbury, two dwellings, which had been built in the second century separated by a wide lane, were later amalgamated into one building, blocking off the lane to the inconvenience of the neighbours.

A house in Insula X at Cirencester (*Corinium Dobunnorum*) closely resembles a winged corridor villa (see Chapter 4). Its frontage was embellished with a projecting portico and to the outside world it must have looked impressive, but its owners were clearly practical working people as behind it lay a workshop in which smithing took place (Wacher 1974, 308). At Silchester, a number of houses had gardens or orchards behind them and corn dryers incorporated into their outbuildings, suggesting that some inhabitants were carrying out farming activities within the town precincts.

It has been suggested that the courtyard house developed from military architecture, as the fully developed peristyle house of the Mediterranean does not appear to have been popular in Britain. A few compact houses at Colchester and Gloucester bear some resemblance to the peristyle form, but the majority of houses in Britain had a more sprawling plan. In Caerwent (*Venta Silurum*), a town on the river Severn which had many veterans from the Second Legion Augusta among its population, the typical house consisted of a square block whose rooms looked inwards to a central courtyard.

The use put to the various rooms in a Romano-British town house is difficult to identify. The main reception rooms are often obvious because of their prominent position and their impressive mosaics and wall paintings, but bedrooms, nurseries, ordinary living rooms, servants' quarters and storerooms are less identifiable. Some town houses, as at Billingsgate, London, had their bathsuites set in a wing of the building, although this is rare as the provision of public bathhouses made having one's own an unnecessary expense in an urban context. Private latrines were more common, often within the house, although latrines might be placed at the bottom of the garden. Rainwater collected from the roof was used to flush domestic latrines, and drinking water was piped by lead or wooden pipes from the town's public water supply on payment of a fee.

The town houses of the wealthy could be very large as a serving magistrate was legally required to live in a house of a specified minimum size. So far, there is no evidence that the apartment blocks to be found in Italian towns of the period were necessary in Britain. Some houses may have had upper storeys to house servants, but most towns were not short of available land, so there was little need to build upwards. The domestic dwellings were rarely arranged with the wealthier inhabitants in one neighbourhood and the poorer elsewhere; the houses of the wealthier merchants and decurions invariably shared blocks with the small shopkeepers and craftsmen. This can be seen from the plan of Silchester (*Calleva Atrebatum*) (see Figure 3), where there are large and small houses jostling together.

In a town, most houses have less outside private space than is the norm in rural areas. In the country, householders become used to using the land around their house for a variety of tasks, even if it is just hanging out the laundry with a reasonable expectation that no one is going to steal it. Those

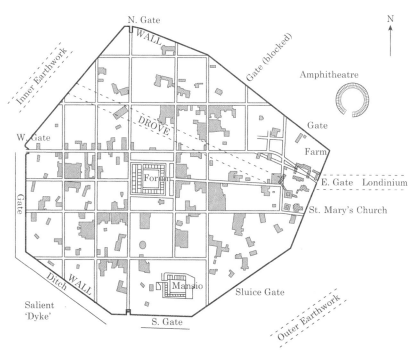

Figure 3 Plan of Silchester.

moving from the country to a Romano-British town may have found the lack of space confining; in particular, many may have experienced storage problems – a small Romano-British town house had a limited area in which to store grain, so most people would have stored only as much as would fit in a grain barrel – rather disconcerting if one had been used to having a whole year's supply available. At Colchester and Leicester, some houses had cellars below ground level to provide extra storage.

Fuel preparation and storage is less of a problem in the country – sources of fuel, such as wood, peat, animal dung or seaweed, are easier to access and there is space to store it; having enough fuel depends on a family's energy and foresight in collecting it. In a Romano-British town, the normal fuel source was charcoal. Town dwellers would not have had the capacity to make their own but would have had to buy it from suppliers. Coal was mostly used in industry or in shrines and temples, although some has been found in domestic and military contexts.

Public buildings

The materials from which their new homes were made were probably a little different to those the incomers were used to. However, there would have been buildings in towns which would have seemed very strange, even frightening, to those newly arrived from the country. Public buildings, such as *fora*, basilicas and temples were usually built of dressed stone and of enormous size. Even people coming from areas where stone was the dominant building material would be unfamiliar with stone being cut with precision to form building blocks and would have been amazed by the sight of pillars, pediments and decorative friezes. But the biggest shock would have been the sheer size of these buildings. Many of the traditional buildings covered a large amount of ground, and their roofs would have reached considerable heights, but they were essentially single-storey buildings with most of their area covered by the slope of their roofs; the new public buildings, with their porticos and columns, would have loomed over passers-by.

The smaller towns had few public buildings, other than temples, and had irregular patterns of streets whose arrangements suggest that they evolved from their position on main roads. Some were simple ribbon developments along a major route; other small towns developed around junctions and had side streets linking the main thoroughfares.

The layout of the larger towns in Roman Britain, however, followed the Mediterranean pattern, with a grid of streets surrounding the centrally placed public buildings. At Silchester, the most extensively excavated Romano-British town, the forum was built around a piazza with its basilica on its west side (see Figure 3). These buildings formed the pivotal point of a Roman town, as it was in the forum that markets were held while the basilica would have been the administrative centre for the town and its surrounding *territorium*. A typical forum was square or rectangular with a series of rooms for offices or commercial outlets arranged along one or three sides of a large central courtyard. At one end was the basilica, which consisted of a large aisled hall in which justice would be meted out by the magistrates who sat on a low stage or tribunal at one or both ends. The hall also accommodated the meetings of the *ordo*. A range of small rooms down the side of the basilica provided offices for the magistrates and their clerks and storage for legal records. Excavations of one of these rooms at Wroxeter (*Viroconium Cornoviorum*) uncovered fragments of wooden office furniture and writing materials. A slightly larger room, often positioned centrally in the range, was probably intended as a shrine.

A town might also have had a separate market building, a *macellum*, in addition to its forum. The *macellum* at Verulamium had two confronting rows of shops with a courtyard between. The third-century *macellum* at Leicester (*Ratae Coritanorum*) consisted of two wings with rows of shops projecting from a building similar to a *basilica* but much smaller and evidently used as a market hall. One room at the Cirencester's *macellum* produced evidence of a butcher's shop.

Many houses had family shrines, intended for private rituals, but those sects which involved congregational worship and required more space were accommodated in large public temples. These were scattered around a town and not confined to a sacred precinct. The proximity of temples with private houses and commercial premises meant that on most days religious processions and the arrival of sacrificial animals on the hoof would have added to the urban cacophony and traffic jams. A massive temple dedicated to the Cult of the Deified Emperors was built at Colchester, largely as a political gesture, but most towns would have had such a temple. Most religious buildings were based on a rectangular plan, often with a *cella* within a surrounding wall, but a variety of plans was used. At Chelmsford (*Caesaromagus*), there was a fourth-century octagonal temple with an apse opposite the entrance to the *cella*, presumably to display the cult figures. At Verulamium, a triangular temple had its apex opposite the gate and appears to have taken its shape from the angle formed by Watling Street and two minor streets.

Some of the larger towns may have been provided with triumphal arches as a reminder to the populace of the power of the emperor. Verulamium is known to have had two monumental arches, which, from their position on the line of the earlier town boundary, may suggest some civic pride on behalf of the townsfolk. In the fourth century, another arch was built across Watling Street, between the theatre and the *macellum*. In the courtyards of the *fora* and other public spaces, imposing statues of emperors or deities may also have been erected by the *ordo* or by individual decurions. In London, the discovery of a section of a massive bronze horse's leg indicates the presence of a large equestrian statue, while a very large human eye also made of bronze, which was found in the *basilica* at Cirencester, presumably came from an imperial statue.

Buildings, similar to modern motels and known as *mansiones*, were built to accommodate official visitors to a town, particularly the staff of the imperial post – the *cursus publicus*. *Mansiones* are to be found in most towns, whether large or small, and were occasionally provided between towns when there was no other accommodation. Within the towns, they were usually situated by one of the main gates. At Silchester, a large building by the south gate has been identified as a *mansio*. This has a central courtyard with three ranges of rooms leading off the corridor which runs around the courtyard. The heated reception rooms were in the west wing. *Mansiones* usually had bathsuites for the use of patrons, and at Silchester this was separated from the main building by an external courtyard.

Although a number of hospitals have been identified in military contexts, no civilian hospitals have been found so far in the towns of Roman Britain. As the military *valetudinaria* have central courtyards surrounded by ranges of rooms, it is possible that some of the courtyard buildings found in towns, which have been identified as private houses or *mansiones*, may actually have been hospitals but no evidence has been uncovered to confirm this. The development of the town at Bath was largely due to the existence of its spa, which provided a medical facility catering for both soldiers and civilians (*RIB* 139, 143–144, 146–147, 152, 156–160), so it is possible that other natural springs were exploited to provide medical facilities and add to the prosperity of other towns.

A burial, c. AD 50–60, found at Stanway near Colchester in 1996 contained 14 surgical instruments as well as other objects which may have had a medical purpose (Jackson 1997). Analysis of these instruments suggests that their owner may have practised medicine before and after the conquest. Whether he was a native Briton or an immigrant from another province is unclear, but his medical equipment suggests that he practised in both pre-Roman British and Mediterranean healing systems. It is possible that he was not attached solely to the invading military but may have been practicing medicine in Britain before the invasion.

A clean and reliable water supply would have been essential if the health of a town's population was to be maintained. Plague regularly broke out throughout the empire, and it is unlikely that Britain escaped. Indeed, John Wacher (1974) has cited epidemics of disease as a contributory factor to the breakdown of Roman Britain in the fifth century AD. The Romans are famous for their engineering feats, and the sewers and aqueducts to be seen across the empire are indeed excellent, the stone-built system of sewers in Lincoln (*Lindum*) being particularly impressive. However, it should be remembered that these monuments were designed merely to keep everything moving, and there was never any method of treating either water or waste. At York, the great sewer uncovered beneath York Minster debouched into the river. In a hot summer, the outfall would be left high and dry on the river bank, resulting in outbreaks of those diseases now known to be carried by foul water and by the insects attracted by foul water. In normal conditions, the waste would enter the river, which was the water supply for several smaller communities downstream. When the water was running fast, oxygen would clean it, but if the water level was low and slow moving, some microbes would survive the journey.

Although most towns had wells, either in public squares or in private gardens, to get an adequate supply of water to an urban population meant that aqueducts had to be built. Examples of urban aqueducts have been investigated at Dorchester, Leicester, Lincoln and Wroxeter, but the evidence of distribution pipes during the excavations of other Romano-British towns suggests that most towns of any size had their water supplied by this means. Given the climate of Britain, the water provided by aqueducts would often have been too little or too much. In the case of drought, there were systems for cutting the water supply off from private dwellings and sending it only to the public reservoirs and fountains; in the case of excess, overflows were directed into the sewers and used to flush them.

The aqueduct at Dorchester was an open, unlined channel with an average width of 1.5 metres and a maximum depth of 0.9 metres. It followed the line of the 91-metre contour with a fall of 7.6 metres over a length of 18.2 kilometres. Wacher (1974, 320) has estimated that it carried nearly 13,000,000 gallons (5,90,99,287 litres) a day to the people of Dorchester. At Lincoln, the water ran underground through pottery pipes, but where it emerged above ground it was carried on an earth bank; as it crossed valleys, it was supported on low masonry piers. Where the water pressure was inadequate, a series of devices was employed; at London, a complicated water-lifting mechanism, based on bucket chains, was found recently, and at Silchester, there was a double-barrelled reciprocating pump with a bore of 76 millimetres. Once in a town, the water was distributed by means of wooden, lead or pottery pipes. Water tanks were also provided to catch and store rainwater.

In Silchester, a large public bathhouse was situated to the south-east of the forum. To the Romans, regular visits to the bathhouse were not just a matter of personal hygiene but a way of meeting friends, relaxing and catching up with gossip. These would have been very busy and noisy places. Wacher (1974) has estimated that the Jewry Wall baths at Leicester would have had to cater for a population of 3,000–4,000; even if each inhabitant contented themselves with just one bath a week, 500 people per day would have had to be accommodated. The excavations at the military bathhouse at the fortress of Caerleon have confirmed that civilian men and women were also welcome, although it is not clear if there were separate times for the military and the townsfolk. This large number of customers meant that a civic bathhouse offered many economic opportunities. Caerleon has shown that the food sellers referred to by Seneca were to be found in British bathing establishments, mostly providing finger food such as chicken legs, lamb chops and oysters (Zienkiewicz 1986; Seneca *Epistulae Morales* 56). The baths at Caerleon have also indicated that a jeweller was working on the premises, while literary sources imply that it was normal to find masseurs, dentists, doctors, beauticians and the repairers of clothes on hand. Cock-fighting bouts were held at Caerleon and Exeter baths, while the number of gaming boards, dice and counters found show that baths also provided a venue for gambling. The discovery of handicraft tools reveals that some women occupied themselves more sedately when bathing.

On arriving at the bathhouse, bathers would first buy an entrance ticket before proceeding to the changing room where they would strip and secure their belongings. The number of curse tablets found in Bath which refer to thefts from the bathhouse suggests that it was a sensible move to pay someone to look after one's possessions, rather than leave them to chance. Once wrapped in a linen towel, it was customary to wash one's face and hands before moving gradually from room to room, each progressively hotter, until a steam room was reached, similar to a modern Turkish bath, where the sweat and dirt were scraped away with a metal implement called a *strigil*. Scented bath oils were used instead of soap. Bathers then entered a hot pool before plunging quickly into a bath of cold water to close their pores. Mixed bathing was banned by law, and the sexes were catered for by separate suites for men and women, children bathing with their mothers.

Other forms of entertainment available in a town would be amphitheatre and theatre performances. Only nine large towns in Britain have, so far, revealed the presence of an amphitheatre, but there is evidence that some small towns, such as the mining settlement at Charterhouse in the Mendips and the religious centre at Frilford, had amphitheatres as well. As these required a large amount of space – the arena at Chichester measured 56 metres by 47 metres – they were usually positioned in the suburbs of a town and were often excluded when the town was enclosed by a protective wall. The amphitheatre at Dorchester utilised a Neolithic henge monument, giving it a nearly circular shape, rather than the oval of a newly built amphitheatre. Unlike the stone structures of the Mediterranean provinces, a British amphitheatre was usually a simple earthen bank, with its entrances and seats made from timber. At Cirencester, the timber amphitheatre was replaced by a masonry structure in the third century.

The discovery of glass and pottery vessels decorated with scenes from the amphitheatre indicates that Britain was familiar with the entertainments offered in the arena. It is likely that the British audiences had to be content with less exotic spectacles than the population in Rome was familiar with, but bear-baiting and bullfights, as well as hand-to-hand combat between people, and public executions, would have been seen (Allason-Jones 2008). The recent excavations at Chester amphitheatre have uncovered many objects – such as a Dragendorff 37 Samian bowl covered in gladiatorial motifs – which might indicate that souvenirs of gladiatorial combat were being sold, just as one can buy souvenirs at a modern sporting venue, although it is also possible that these were used for the gladiators' meal (*cena libera*) held before the games. Admission to an amphitheatre was free, but a small lead disc found at Caerleon, stamped with the letters 'XIII' within a triangle, may tell us that tickets were used to allocate seats (Zienkiewicz 1986, 26–27). It has also been suggested that some of the small incised discs of bone and pottery, which have been found on many sites in Britain, could have been used as seating tickets for both the arena and the theatre.

Theatres are known at Canterbury, Colchester and Gosbecks Farm, but the best surviving is to be seen at Verulamium (see Illustration 10). Originally built in the first century AD as an adjunct to a temple, the theatre had a central orchestra with a stage and integral scenery on its north-west edge. The audience was seated on raked wooden seating, supported by an earth bank and reached by wooden staircases against the outer walls. More commonly, theatres were semicircular in shape and the circular arrangement at Verulamium suggests that it was also used as an amphitheatre. For a few performances some members of the audience would have had to put up with a restricted view of the stage.

Many plays have survived from Roman times to give us a flavour of the theatrical entertainment on offer, but it is not known how often these were performed in Britain or if British theatregoers were familiar with the full repertoire. On the stage, masks were used by the actors to identify their characters; an ivory tragic mask found at Caerleon and the pottery masks from Baldock and Catterick may suggest that bands of travelling players brought popular productions to rural or military areas. That there were people deeply interested in the theatre in Britain may be inferred from a room with a painting of tragic masks in a house at Leicester and a garnet intaglio, incised with an actor's mask, which was found in a gold ring from Housesteads.

Despite the encouragement of wealthy citizens, such as Marcus Ulpius Januarius at Brough-on-Humber (*RIB* 707), to pay for theatre buildings or theatrical performances, the status of an actor was not high and persons of quality who appeared on the stage did so at the risk of losing their standing in society. In Britain, a fragment of pottery graffiti links Verecunda, an actress, with Lucius, a gladiator, both of whom would have been considered to be of low social status.

One major advantage of urban living in the Roman period was access to a range of local and imported commodities. Besides the markets held in the forum and the *macellum*, there would also be many shops, a number of which have been excavated at Verulamium and Wroxeter. Each shop would have offered a limited stock, usually the product of the shop owner. Two shops at Castleford and Lancaster sold only *mortaria*. Goldsmiths are known to have been working at Verulamium, London, Cirencester and Norton. A glassmaker worked from one of the rooms in the market hall at Leicester, although not entirely legally as apparently he was also melting silver coins to recover their silver content (Wacher 1974, 65). Wine merchants are known at York and Lincoln, but there must have been several in most towns of any size. Merchants and traders would have visited, bringing with them jewellery from the Continent, olive oil from Spain, wines from Africa, Spain and Gaul, fish sauce from Spain and Tunisia, and even doum palm from Palestine (Tomlin 2003b). Britain offered a new market for foreign goods, and many traders, such as Marcus Verecundius Diogenes from Bourges (*RIB* 678), were quick to exploit it.

Any town with a river or coastal frontage would have had wharves and warehouses. The wharf uncovered at Gloucester, for example, shows how vital the river Severn was to the economy of the town. The warehouses in the first century were of timber, but a more substantial stone harbour was added later. The port at London must have been extremely busy if the quantity and size of the wooden warehousing excavated there and the range of artefacts found are any indication.

Defences

Few towns had defensive walls in the first century AD as, at that time, these could only be erected with the express permission of the emperor. By the end of the second century, however, towns of all sizes and even villages had been provided with fortified perimeter walls and defensible gateways. Many of these walls were simply earth ramparts, but by the mid-third century, previously undefended towns were being surrounded by walls built of stone. By the fourth century, all urban conurbations had a defensive circuit. In the years following the Barbarian Conspiracy of 367, external interval towers were added to the curtain walls of the major centres, implying that the townsfolk were expected to play a part in defending themselves with artillery; alternatively, the towers may be taken as evidence for the presence of military units in the towns.

Although a town with a perimeter wall needs gates to allow its residents and traders easy access, it is clear that the town gates were built with defence in mind. Several of these gates, as at Caister-by-Norwich, had flanking towers and guard rooms, but their size may also have been intended to reflect civic pride – the *ordo*, after all, would have had to pay for them. A number of town gates of Roman date still survive to be seen today, a good example being the Newport Arch at Lincoln.

People

The population of a town would have been a mixture of local people and incomers, free, freed and slaves. At Dorchester (Dorset), Carinus, husband of Romana and father of a son and two daughters, is recorded on his tombstone as a Roman citizen; this public declaration may imply that he was a local man who had gained citizenship, rather than someone who had been born a citizen (*RIB* 188). His neighbours, however, may have come from anywhere in the empire and be of any legal status.

Racial prejudice does not appear to have been a problem in the Roman Empire. As long as a person was from the Roman Empire, they were acceptable; if they came from outside the frontier, they were regarded as barbarians. The emperors themselves came from all over the world: Septimius Severus, for example, was a Libyan, and there is no suggestion in the literature of the time that the colour of someone's skin was any more than part of their physical description. However, individuals react to other individuals in their own way: someone whose experience of skin tone variation has been confined to the pasty or ruddy hues of a northerner may not react to other skin colours in the broad-minded way of a sophisticated Roman citizen. There is evidence that there were tensions between people from the different provinces. The Vindolanda writing tablet, for example, which refers to *Brittunculi* – 'wretched little Britons' – may suggest that Britons were not always held in high regard (*Tab. Vindol.* 164).

Tensions between groups of people were always present, and this may have led to trouble. Gaius Severius Emeritus, centurion of the region, who restored at Bath 'this holy spot, wrecked by insolent hands and cleansed afresh' (*RIB* 152), may have been clearing up after a spate of violence or possibly after mindless vandalism. In these situations, privacy and the ability to lock one's door become important – it is noticeable that whereas the Iron Age had its simple latch lifters, complex locks and keys only became commonplace once the Romans had arrived.

Besides immigrants coming to the country to seek their fortune, skilled individual craftsmen are known to have moved from town to town within the province to improve their earning capacity. C. Attius Marinus, for example, was a potter who began his working life in Colchester but then moved on to Radlett near St Albans before finishing his career in the flourishing pottery production centre at Hartshill in Warwickshire. Other artisans would have found it profitable to travel from town to town continually, selling their wares, if they traded in luxury goods.

In Roman Britain, there would have been migrants from all over the Roman world and each person would have had a different experience. For some Britons, the differences between their agricultural origins and the new life in a town or city would have been overwhelming. For most native Britons, the sense of being a foreigner in their own land must have led to a great deal of stress and distress. One's upbringing has a great deal to do with how one reacts to crowds. Those brought up in a bustling urban environment probably do not mind being with lots of people, indeed may thrive on it, but for those raised in small, quiet, firmly structured communities, the noise and chaos of crowds might be very stressful. If the newcomers found themselves living in an overcrowded tenement or street where there was no escape, then real psychological problems may have developed. In Roman Britain, in the first century AD, there were many people who were experiencing crowds for the first time. If you add the fact that Britain was now under an occupying power, that a new language had become more important than the native languages, that a person had to be able to read and write to be successful, that Britain was now a monetary economy and that knowledge of specific time had become an essential factor in the smooth running of the province, one begins to feel that life in a Romano-British town may have been extremely stressful.

Chapter 4
Country Life

In Britain, as elsewhere in the world, the rural population throughout the centuries has been inclined to resist change unless they can see obvious benefits in the new ways, and this appears to have been particularly true in the Roman period. Evidence across the country suggests that the Roman invasion had less initial impact on the agricultural communities, at least those outside the immediate area of the invasion, than might have been expected. Indeed, it is quite likely that many people living on isolated farms in the north and west of the country may have been unaware for some years after the invasion that they had become absorbed into the Roman Empire.

During the Early Iron Age, the people of Britain lived mostly in circular houses in hillforts or small open settlements with associated field systems, but by the first century BC, it became more common for the agricultural communities to live in farmsteads surrounded by a ditch and bank or stone wall enclosure. Very often, these occupation sites contained a single dwelling with associated animal pens and produce stores, but some have been found with as many as sixteen houses within one enclosure, probably housing related families. The material used for the buildings would have depended on the underlying geology. Where there was plenty of suitable stone, boulders or roughly hewn blocks were used, although without any bonding matrix. Elsewhere wood, wattle-and-daub or clay was used. Equally, the roofing materials would have depended on whatever was to hand: straw, reed, heather or wooden slats. These were not small houses, some have been found with a diameter of 40 feet (12.19 metres), and it is probable that they provided accommodation for extended families, with several generations living under one roof. Such settlements continued to be occupied well into the Roman period, as late as the third century AD in some more remote regions.

The people who lived in these rural communities would mostly have been related to each other. Newcomers would have been introduced by marriage, but most newcomers were likely to have come from similar settlements in the surrounding district and would have been familiar with the way of life in their new home. An individual's status in the group would have depended on their age, sex and relationship to the dominant adult, but this hierarchy would have been clearly understood, without any need for explanation. No person living in such a settlement would have had any doubt as to how they fitted in, and everyone would have worked at producing, gathering and processing food, regardless of age or sex.

Everyone living in the settlement would have spoken the same language. Newcomers may have introduced different dialect terms or those idiosyncratic words which exist in most close-knit families and which are unintelligible to outsiders, but a new bride or groom or a passing traveller would have had no difficulty in making themselves immediately understood in day-to-day conversations; the only difficulty may have been different, possibly quite strong, accents.

Everyone in the settlement would have been encouraged to hold similar religious beliefs. There may have been different rites for women and men, for young and old, but there would have been recognised feast days which would have been celebrated by all those inhabitants who were qualified to do so by sex or age. The inhabitants would have had a shared history which would have been passed on through the generations by stories told on feast days or on long winter evenings. It is probably going too far to claim that everyone in the settlement would have had the same sense of humour, but it is possible that they would all have had a common value system, sharing the same sense of what was important and what was trivial, what was right and what was wrong, and whose responsibility it was to do certain tasks.

The yearly cycle of such a settlement would have been punctuated by religious festivals, many of which would have been tied to the agricultural seasons. Indeed, life in general would have been closely tied to nature as the occupants would have mostly relied on what they were able to grow, hunt or gather for their food supply and this would have depended on the time of year and the weather. The aim of such a community would have been to amass enough food to feed the group and allow some surplus to be stored for next year's seeds or against a potentially bad year, as well for trading with others.

This sketch of life in an Iron Age/early-Roman-period settlement may be over generalised, may rely too much on anthropological comparisons and may be coloured by the author's own observations during her childhood in an agricultural community, as well as her experiences while working in countries such as Sudan and Libya, but it seems to be the general view of the situation. From the time that the population of Britain ceased to be purely hunters and gatherers and became agriculturalists, living in settled communities and using methods of farming which lent themselves to the support of small groups of people, whether those people lived in villages or scattered farmsteads, the group dynamics of agricultural village life would have become the norm. Except for those people living on the coast who had access to fishing or merchant trading with their maritime neighbours, this was a way of life which would have been commonplace for the majority of Britons until the Romans arrived and for several generations afterwards.

The impact of the invasion

The invading Roman army was aware that the land they were coming to had a rich farming tradition which was capable of producing a surplus. Indeed, Strabo's reference to Britain's exports of grain and cattle may have been a contributory factor to Julius Caesar's and Claudius's decisions to invade; an empire with a large army would always require access to sustainable food supplies, and when invading a potential province, it was important to have adequate sources of grain and meat to hand (Caesar *De Bello Gallico* 5.12; Strabo *Geography* 4.199). The invasion, and the Roman advance through the country, would initially have had an adverse effect as battles were fought over fields, and crops and settlements were destroyed by enemy action, but it would have been to the Romans' advantage to ensure that the local agricultural rhythms were quickly re-established. As the province became more settled and the population rose through the influx of troops, merchants and other travellers, plus an expansion in the proportions of less productive town dwellers, the need for higher yields would have become evident and the shrewder farmers would have adjusted their arable and animal production to take advantage of the situation.

One early impact of the Roman invasion is likely to have been on the demographics of the rural population. During the Iron Age, a young man would have aimed at becoming a warrior and worked on his fighting skills, even if most of his life was connected to agriculture. Having an established warrior class within their new province would not have suited the Roman government, and fit young men would have been encouraged to join the Roman army to keep them from forming viable resistance movements. As discussed in Chapter 2, it was more common for British recruits in the early period to be posted to other provinces than serve in Britain, so large-scale recruitment would have effectively cut the available agricultural workforce, just at a time when more food was required.

Another effect may have been the confiscation of land as the initial fighting or later rebellions, such as that of Boudicca, led to property being annexed for the emperor. A brisk decision would have had to have been made by the tribal aristocracy when the Romans first appeared in an area as to whether they would defy the invaders and risk losing their lands or accept Roman rule with all the limitations and tax implications that this carried. Anthony Birley has suggested that following the activities of potential usurpers, such as Albinus in AD 195–197 and Carausius and Allectus between AD 287 and 296, their supporters would also have found their lands taken as punishment, as was usual Roman practice in such circumstances (Birley 1979). The appearance of an official known as the *rationalis rei privatae per Britannias*, or administrator, of the emperor's private estates in Britain in the *Notitia Dignitatum*, would suggest that there were official imperial estates in Britain, although the location of most is unknown. A building inscription found at Combe Down in Somerset mentions a procurator's assistant called Naevius, an imperial freedman, who was responsible for restoring 'from ground level these ruined Headquarters' (*RIB* 179); as no fort has been discovered in the area, it might be postulated that the headquarters referred to are those of an imperial estate; a similar identification has been suggested for the tower building at Stonea Grange in the Fens (Jackson and Potter 1996).

Not all those farming the land during the Roman period had done so from birth. In the early years of the Roman occupation, it was still the norm for retiring soldiers to be given a plot of land. In the case of Colchester, the land confiscated from the royal estates of Cunobelin may have been divided up and given to the veterans who were being settled at Colchester; this has been identified as one of the factors contributing to the ill feeling that developed between the locals and the veterans and led to the Boudiccan revolt (Salway 1981, 103–104). It is possible that a region known as *Bremetenacum Veteranorum* near Ribchester in Lancashire was also a veteran settlement, farmed by soldiers who had served their twenty-five years in the army and decided to settle close to their last posting (*RIB* 587). Some of these old soldiers might have come from agricultural backgrounds and known how to get the best out of their land; others might not and would have had to sell up when their farms failed.

Farmhouses

Through the first century AD, the need for more food led to changes in the layout and architecture of the farms. Today, we refer to all farms built during the Roman period as villas, but it is unclear if this term was actually used in Britain for every farm. In Italy, the word was used for any rural establishment, from the most basic farmstead to the large landed estates of senators, but it may be that in the north-west provinces it was only used in association with the larger properties. It is also a term which applies mostly to sites south of a line from the Humber to the Severn; north of this line, very few villas have been identified, although some have been found as far north as Old Durham and Old Quarry Farm in Cleveland.

Some villas were built to replace an Iron Age roundhouse, but it is difficult to be sure whether these were erected by the original families or by incomers. There are some sites where the new building overlies the actual site of the roundhouse and this may indicate that the farm had been abandoned before new people, with more modern ideas, took over; on others, the roundhouse went on being used while newer buildings were built close by. The new ideas as to the layout of a farmhouse took a variety of forms but all involved the major change from living in a circular building to occupying a rectangular one, although it is possible that this change had already started before the invasion. The simplest farmhouses were rectangular, aisled buildings in which the occupants appear to have lived communally, as they had done in the roundhouses, and it is possible that the buildings also housed stock and provided space for storing equipment and produce. As they became more established, partitions were built to divide the hall into separate rooms. Sometimes these aisled farmhouses were well appointed; at Sparsholt, for example, two rooms were decorated with mosaic floors and wall paintings, and a bathsuite was built in one corner. At first, this bathsuite only had a portable bath and its underfloor heating system was used occasionally as a corn dryer, but it is clear that the occupants had some knowledge of the Roman way of life and wished to follow it.

On most farm sites, the aisled farmhouses did not provide the principal accommodation for long. Many were replaced or augmented by buildings that an Italian visitor would recognise as a small villa: single storey, rectangular buildings, sometimes with a verandah along one long face. At Frocester (Gloucestershire), the earliest villa had a large central room flanked at its south-west end by a smaller room, with a corridor and another room at its north-east end. In many villas, a central front door led from the verandah to the main room, from which the flanking rooms could be accessed. Like the roundhouses, these simple villas were built of the locally available building materials: wattle-and-daub, wood or clay on rough stone foundations, some had tiled or slate roofs but many would have continued to use the traditionally preferred thatching material. On a number of farms, for example Brading (Isle of Wight) and Llantwit Major (Glamorgan), the aisled building continued to be occupied even after a Mediterranean-type villa building was erected next door; at others, such as Spoonley Wood and Hartlip, the aisled buildings were relegated to barns.

The adoption of what might be seen as classic villa architecture may suggest incoming people or incoming ideas but may also reflect a growing desire for separation between the farm owner's family and its workforce. Some villas never progressed beyond this stage, and it is to be presumed that the acreage and productivity of the land under cultivation or pasture controlled how much profit could be made and thus how elaborate a farmhouse could become.

The basic corridor villa sometimes expanded into, or was replaced by, the winged corridor villa, an architectural development which was also seen in the towns in the second century AD. At Lockleys, this was achieved by building a corridor along the front of the five existing rooms, which linked projecting extensions at both ends; this suggests occupation by a family with a modest amount of spare cash which they preferred to expend on their living accommodation rather than on improving stock or buying more land. It is not always possible to ascertain if these buildings had upper storeys, but at Lockleys, a two-storey block has been identified at one corner, although this seems to have been a remedy for counteracting the slope of the land and Lockleys might be more properly described as a split-level dwelling rather than a two-storey one. More rooms and a second corridor might also be added if there was a need for more space.

The largest and most elaborate villa type, usually with the most impressive interior decoration, was the courtyard villa. As the name suggests, it had several ranges of rooms set out around three or four sides of a central courtyard or garden. Occasionally, this courtyard enclosed barns and other farm buildings, but in the largest, such as Bignor (Sussex), a second enclosure was built onto the first to separate the farm

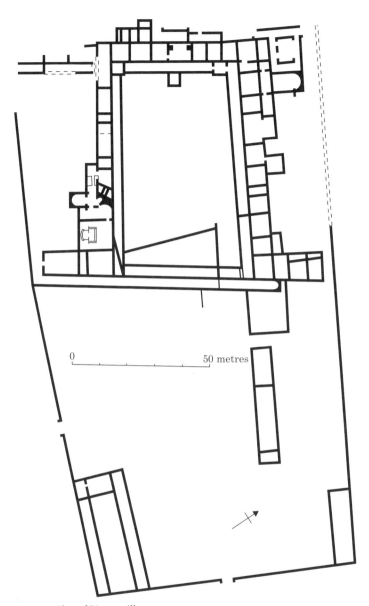

Figure 4 Plan of Bignor villa.

buildings from the main occupation building (see Figure 4). The
excavations at Bignor revealed that there was originally a simple, timber-
framed strip house on the site, which was burnt down in the early years
of the third century. This was replaced by an equally simple rectangular
stone building which was gradually extended, first into a winged corridor

77

villa with its bathsuite and piped water and finally into a palatial courtyard layout with at least forty-six rooms, mostly linked by a corridor which ran round the courtyard. Despite its elaborate design, Bignor was always a single-storey dwelling with occasional short flights of steps to accommodate the south-facing slope.

On the evidence of sites such as Bignor, it is tempting to see the various designs of villas as representing a chronological and financial development from roundhouse to aisled building, to strip villa, then winged corridor villa before finishing up with the courtyard villa, but this is to oversimplify a complicated situation. The different styles of farmhouse building on a single site might have followed this progression, but this was rare and the different types were built on new sites throughout the centuries. The earliest winged corridor villas, for example, have been dated to the second century AD, but at Mansfield Woodhouse an example was built in the third century while the villa at Great Staughton (Cambridgeshire) suggests that the style was still popular in the fourth century. The type of house built, or any improvements made to an existing house, would largely have depended on the resources of its owners and their family's needs and expectations.

The occupants of these simple farms would have had busy lives which probably differed little from those of their Iron Age predecessors, in that the whole household would have been involved in the work of the farm and their year would have been regulated by the changes in the seasons. Annual success and continued or growing prosperity would have depended on hard work, the weather and a certain amount of good luck.

The occupants of the larger villa estates, on the other hand, would have been less reliant on agriculture than those in the smaller strip villas. As the simple farms grew larger, their owners' interests and horizons would have changed; the proprietor of Bignor in the fourth century, for example, could never have sustained such a massive establishment on the proceeds of agriculture alone, no matter how large the estate was, and must have been involved in profitable activities elsewhere. Many courtyard villas will have provided rural retreats for aristocrats and officials, whose political and financial life would have been centred on the towns, and it is probable that the families spent more time at their town houses. Yet, despite its elaborate layout, Bignor still retained its agricultural raison d'être, and there were barns, granaries and animal byres in the outer courtyard.

Country people

A large staff of slaves and freed servants would have been required
to ensure the smooth running of such an establishment; indeed, on the
larger estates, the population may have exceeded that of an average
village. A complicated hierarchy of slaves and freed servants would have
been common. At the top, there would have been a steward to run the
house and another to run the agricultural aspects of the estate. Below
them, there would have been a range of people with different levels
of responsibility. There is evidence that slaves could in their turn own
slaves: a writing tablet from London of the late first or early second
century reveals a complicated sliding scale of slavery as it describes
the sale of a female slave to 'Vegetus, assistant slave of Montanus, the
slave of the August Emperor and sometime assistant slave of Iucundus'
(Tomlin 2003a, 41–51); at the top of this chain is a slave in the imperial
employ, but similar scales of ownership would have been common on the
larger estates with some slaves working solely on the farm while some
household servants would have accompanied their owners on their
travels between their country and town houses.

It cannot be presumed that every farm was worked by an owner-
occupier. Some larger landowners would have had stewards running farms
on their behalf or have had tenant farmers renting the land and buildings
from them. In the case of an Italian heiress called Melania, it is known
that she owned extensive estates in Britain, but it is not known if she ever
visited them or had any involvement in their running. It must be presumed
that she had agents who oversaw her properties and tenant farmers whose
rents added to her annual income (*Vita Melania* 10).

Few villa owners or occupiers are known by name due to a lack
of inscriptions from rural sites in Britain, except on the occasions when
a villa had a private burial plot. At Branston, for example, Aurelia
Concessa, 'a very pure girl', was buried 'on the estate' (Moore 1975);
it has been presumed that she was the daughter of the estate owner.
In Wiltshire, the discovery at Studley of tiles marked *Iuc Dig* suggests
that one estate was owned by a man called Juc(undius) Dignus who
found it worthwhile to produce his own building materials (*RIB*
2489.18). Not all these villa owners were of British origins; Anthony
Birley has identified Termo at Wanborough (*Durocornovium*) as a
Greek while Maecius, Maxima and Ingenuus at Springhead and
Antonius and Campana at Chilham have all been identified as

immigrants by their names (Birley 1979, 138–139). One landowner, Quintus Natalius Natalinus, also known as Bodenus, whose name appears on a mosaic at his villa at Thruxton, Hampshire, is likely to have been a Briton who acquired a new Roman name as his fortunes prospered (*RIB* 2448.9). The names of two estates have been identified by Applebaum (1972): Anicetis and Coloneas, the first apparently named after a Greek, Quintus Pompeius Anicetus, who dedicated at the Temple of Sulis at Bath (*RIB* 148), while Coloneas may have come from the name of a British landowner called Colon or Colonus. Applebaum has further suggested that Anicetis could have been a *conductor* or someone who rented lands on an imperial estate.

Many of the people identified by Birley (1979) as country dwellers are only known by names appearing on spoons, religious plaques, statuettes or other transportable items; so it is difficult to be sure if they actually lived in the local villa and, if they did, whether they were the owner, one of the family or simply part of the staff structure. Even when a name is recorded on the building, we cannot be sure who the name belonged to; at Barnsley Park, for example, the name Firminius appears on a building stone, but is this the name of the owner or a building contractor (Wright 1968)?

Owning land under Roman rule involved administration and bureaucracy. A writing tablet found at Chew Stoke, Somerset, records the purchase of land by someone whose name has been read as Marcus Aurelius Riespetecus and uses formulaic phrases to assert that the estate is 'free from servitudes'; such documents must have been commonplace throughout the province as land and homes changed hands (Turner 1956).

In some areas, the difference in lifestyles between those who lived in the country and those who lived in the towns must have been very small. Many town sites have produced pig bones, which suggest that the Mediterranean habit of keeping a pig in the backyard was not unusual in Britain, and many houses had gardens large enough to grow some vegetables. Some small farmers whose land was close to the expanding towns may have lived within the limits of the town and gone out to tend their fields and livestock each day.

Few farms concentrated on producing just one type of crop or rearing a single breed of animal; the majority would have had a mixture of cows, pigs and sheep with crops, including cereals, vegetables and fruit, grown for consumption by the farm's occupants and for sale, as well as for animal fodder. The seasonal round would have involved preparing the ground for crops, sowing and harvesting as well as the various annual tasks involved in animal husbandry, such as sheep shearing. Daily life would have included feeding the animals and attending to the beehives, as well as hoeing and weeding, keeping the tools and fences in order and gathering wild food to augment the diet. Shepherds and cowherds may have been employed to look after flocks and herds on pastures some distance from the main farm. Evidence from the Vindolanda writing tablets shows that, despite Caesar's assertion that the British kept hens and geese as pets rather than for their eggs or meat, poultry farming had become widespread (*Tab. Vindol.* 302). Both Varro and Columella were of the opinion that a flock of 200 hens was all a single poultry keeper could cope with, 'provided, however, that an industrious old woman or a boy is laid on to watch out for those that stray' (Varro *De Re Rustica* III.9; Columella *De Re Rustica* VIII.2.2–2.7). Children and the elderly also would have played a part in scaring birds away from the crops.

Agricultural improvements

The building of an extensive network of roads and bridges, initially to expedite the movement of troops, would have allowed the larger landowners to travel comfortably from their villas to their town houses, while also offering farmers the means of getting their produce to markets, linking them more efficiently with their customers. In the Yorkshire Wolds near Hayton, excavation and survey have shown that the building of the road from Brough-on-Humber (*Petuaria*) to York altered the orientation of the landscape as far as the local inhabitants were concerned, as it became easier to transport goods to other settlements in the neighbourhood or to the expanding city of York, even to the port at Brough for export. A line of roadside settlements offered comforts and stopping places en route.

Whether it was the large landowners or the small farmers or the demands of the army that drove the agricultural improvements, it is clear that the four centuries of Roman rule saw several important developments in both arable and livestock husbandry. One of the earliest that can be observed is an increase in the size of cattle, followed by a similar increase in the size of sheep. This must have been the result of deliberate programmes of improved breeding, possibly cross-breeding with imported animals, and/or regimes of improved feeding. In arable farming, discernible changes can also be seen which would have increased yields. In some areas, such as the Fens, there is evidence of drainage programmes which brought marginal land into cultivation.

Environmental sampling has indicated a growing emphasis on bread wheat on the better arable lands close to towns but with distinct regional variations developing, with rye and millet in the east of the country and oats and barley in the north. There is also evidence that larger fields were preferred, and that market gardening for profit rather than just home consumption became more common. Certainly, some vegetable crops, such as leeks and carrots, made their appearance for the first time during the Roman period, and this would have had an impact on the landscape as well as on the growing practices of the rural population.

There has been much debate over the years as to whether the Romans introduced viticulture to Britain. The evidence from Iron Age sites in the south-east make it clear that wine as a commodity was known and appreciated for many years before the invasion, but this evidence is largely in the form of amphorae that would have been used to transport the wine from the Continent. No evidence has come to light of the pre-Roman population growing grapes and making their own wine, but excavations at Woollaston near Peterborough have revealed unequivocal evidence of a Roman period vineyard. The vines were planted 1.5 metres apart in trenches and trained along wooden trellises, following a method of vine cultivation known as *pastinatio* to Columella and Pliny (*Naturalis Historia* XVII.166). It has been estimated that the Woollaston vineyard would have produced over 10,500 litres of white wine per year. Other vineyards have been suggested on the sites at neighbouring Grendon, North Thoresby in Lincolnshire, and Gloucester.

There is a great deal of literary evidence for both private and commercial beekeeping during the Roman period from writers such as Virgil, Columella and Varro (*Georgics* 4; *De Re Rustica* 9.2–9.16; *De Re Rustica* 3.1.6). Beehives of Roman date which have been found elsewhere in the empire were made of wood or straw, neither of which are likely to have survived in Britain, or of pottery, such as at Sphakia in south-west Crete, where they are known from distinctive rim fragments. Sadly, there is some doubt as to the identification of some pottery fragments from the south of Britain at Casterley Camp and Rockbourne Villa which have been cautiously identified as beehive rims.

Tools

During the Iron Age, there had been a continuing improvement in the tools available for the farmer to use and these developments continued throughout the Roman period. These improvements are most noticeable in the ploughs. During the first century BC, and all through the Roman occupation, the iron tips covering the ends of wooden ploughshares lengthened until the whole share was made of iron. This change can be seen on ards which cut through the soil but do not turn the earth over, as well as on ploughs, which have a mouldboard capable of turning the cut turf or soil. The development may have been because of the increasing availability of iron, but its effect would have been the improved efficiency and quality of ards and ploughs. There were also developments in the coulters, the iron cutters in front of a ploughshare, with the result that the average plough increased in weight and improved in design becoming capable of tilling heavier soils in larger fields (Rees forthcoming). The design of the late-Roman ploughshares from Folkestone, Brading and Dinorben shows that the ploughs probably had a fixed mouldboard and were heavy enough to allow for the cultivation of almost any soil type, including heavy clays. On the evidence of a small bronze model found in Sussex, some ploughs also appear to have had earthboards attached which would cover the seed after it had been broadcast (Manning 1964). All these slight changes would have made a great difference to the workload of a farmer; instead of having to cross-plough several times with an ard to break up the ground sufficiently, then sow and cover the seed, a farmer would now need to plough a field only once and could sow and cover in one operation.

In smaller fields or in market gardens, hoes and mattocks would have been used to break up the soil. These rarely appear in pre-Roman contexts, but a range of versions was used from the first century AD onwards. Tools such as mattocks, adzes, turfcutters and *dolabrae* may have been introduced by the military as they would have been required to clear land for forts and for establishing frontier lines or temporary camps. Those veterans who had been allotted or had acquired land would have been comfortable using such equipment, and its versatility would have been evident to their farming neighbours.

It is probable that some of the sophisticated agricultural equipment described by the classical writers was used on British farms. A harrow for soil preparation or for covering seed, consisting of a wooden frame with iron teeth, is described by Varro (*De Re Rustica* 5.136) and may be an interpretation of the 16 'rake-prongs' found at Walbrook, London. Some tools which had specifically agricultural purposes, such as the *ascia-rastrum* hoe which was used for careful weeding and for soil aeration, must have been introduced by those who had knowledge of farming practice in the Mediterranean regions. Hoes which can be identified as being of the *ascia-rastrum* type are confined to town sites, forts and small settlements but, curiously, rarely appear on villas (Rees forthcoming), a distribution which is mirrored in that of a heavier, double-tined hoe of the type called a *bidens* by the classical writers (Pliny *Naturalis Historia* 1.54, 18.46; Columella *De Re Rustica* 4.5.1, 4.10.1, 5.9.12). Evidence for the use of the *vallus*, a complicated machine with iron teeth, pushed by oxen and used for harvesting grain, has so far eluded archaeologists in Britain. Its description in the works of classical agronomists, such as Pliny (*Naturalis Historia* 18.296) and Palladius (*On Husbandrie* 7.2.2–7.2.4), however, indicates that it was a machine with many individual parts, so that identifying with certainty any fragment of wood or shaped piece of iron as a piece of a vallus is extremely difficult.

The most commonly found digging tools are spades, or rather the iron sheaths that protected the cutting edge of a wooden spade. These were used for a variety of agricultural and non-agricultural purposes and are found on military and town sites as well as villas and small farms. It has been suggested that the practice of shoeing a spade with iron was introduced into Britain at the beginning of the Roman period. A spade from Blackburn Mill with its entire back covered in iron and with a footrest to one side of the handle has been identified as a peat cutter; its discovery, as well as the discovery of axes, on many rural sites is a reminder that, whereas a town dweller might have charcoal delivered to his home, country dwellers would have had to ensure their own fuel supplies. Wood for building and for fuel was an important cash crop, and careful pollarding and coppicing would have ensured sustainable supplies of the materials needed for building wattle-and-daub structures, for fencing hurdles, basketry and charcoal. The amount of charcoal required as fuel for cooking and industry may suggest that many farmers would have found profit in this seasonal occupation.

There were also changes in the tools used for harvesting crops. During the Iron Age, the preferred harvesting tool was the sickle, which allows

the grain to be cut single handedly at any height of stalk, and examples
have been found which indicate that the sickle went on being used, with
little alteration to its design, throughout the Roman period, although
the Roman examples do tend to have greater balance and more elegant
blades. However, alternative harvesting equipment is found in increasing
numbers as the period progresses. Reaping hooks, for example, appear
with a variety of curved blades, suggesting that users would make or buy
hooks with specific tasks in mind, such as harvesting non-cereal crops
or cutting thatching materials or animal fodder. The scythe has been
assumed to be a Roman military introduction for cutting horse fodder
as the earliest examples found in the province have been discovered
at forts, such as Newstead, Brampton and Bar Hill. Very large scythes,
up to 160 centimetres in length, have been found at Barnsley Park and
Farmoor, among other civilian sites, and these were used for hay cutting,
a practice that was either introduced by the Romans or greatly developed
by them. That these were prized tools can be presumed by the number
of careful repairs that are visible on many examples.

Harvesting tools require constant sharpening if they are to be effective.
Mowers' anvils were used for sharpening blades in the field, and the
Roman examples were exactly the same as those in the nineteenth and
early twentieth century whose use was described by Curle in 1911:
'The mower sits on the ground and laying the scythe across his knees,
hammers out the edges on the anvil planted between his legs before
giving the edge a final polish with a hone' (Curle 1911, 284). Stones
would be placed under the anvils to stop them sinking into the ground
while in use. Curle's description, in association with the harvesting tools
found on Roman sites, such as pitchforks and rakes, draws a picture
of Romano-British harvesting which must have differed little from rural
scenes in the eighteenth and nineteenth centuries until the introduction
of the combined harvester.

Several tools, including curved blades, angled blades and saws, have
been found which will have been used in the care of fruit trees. There were
plenty of fruit trees in Britain in the Iron Age, but it is true to say that
several new species and several improvements on native species of fruit
were introduced by the Romans. For example, the native gean cherry
(*Prunus avium*) was exploited in the first century BC, but the sour cherry
(*Prunus cerasus*) begins to appear in the archaeological record in the
second century AD. It is possible that the newer cherries were imported
already bottled, but the discovery of seeds of mulberries and medlars in

south-west Britain, fruit which does not travel well, indicates that these were being cultivated in the country. Aerial photographs of villa sites, such as Ditchley (Oxfordshire), suggest that many had orchards, while the discovery of the tools necessary for pruning and husbanding fruit reveals an understanding of how to maximise fruit crops.

Rural industry

Not all rural communities were purely agricultural, although most would have carried out enough agricultural activity to maintain a basic food supply for their inhabitants. There has been a tendency for archaeologists to refer to pre-Roman agricultural groupings as 'settlements' while using the term 'village' when discussing post-invasion clusters of rural dwellings. This differentiation has been based on the presumption that in the pre-Roman period, the settlement dwellers concentrated on food production and any industrial activity was solely for home consumption, while in the Roman period, a higher proportion of the rural population, outside the villas, was involved in other activities. It is now known that the Iron Age farmers were involved in a wide range of non-agricultural activities, such as salt production, and that many later villas had industrial interests to support their farming activities, so this differentiation does not always stand up to scrutiny. However we may define the term, in the first century AD villages – in the sense of settlements which are larger than single family farms – began to be built in the south-east, with the houses following the urban trend to rectangular dwellings, first of wood and wattle-and-daub, later of stone. These small villages tended to develop on sites which had had some Iron Age occupation; in most cases, there is no evidence for an influx of new people, merely a change in the layout of the villages. Other villages developed in areas with the natural resources required for mining or pottery production, such a Little Down (Avon), where pewter and iron goods were made for the markets in nearby Bath. Some villages, such as Catsgore in Somerset, became prosperous with large, well-appointed houses, or expanded in size until, as at Chalton (Hampshire), they covered as much as 17 acres (6.88 hectares) and verged on becoming small towns.

Some villages grew up along the coast and seem to have had only the slightest links with agriculture, their existence being associated with fishing, the exploitation of oyster beds and the production of salt. Letter 593 at Vindolanda indicates that a range of nets was available, some for catching thrushes or ducks, but dragnets for fishing are also listed. These might explain the lack of metal fish hooks in Romano-British assemblages, although they are common from sites around the Mediterranean. The British oyster industry took off during the governorship of Agricola. To start with, the natural beds along the Kent coast were exploited, but as demand, both within the province and in the rest of the empire, outstripped supply artificial beds were introduced and whole communities must have been involved in collecting, packing and transporting these delicacies. More prosaically, but probably just as profitably, there is evidence that salt production was already well established around the coast and in the Fens in the first century BC and the need for salt for hide preparation, cooking, food preservation and medicines would have become even more important during the Roman period. At Canvey Island, the spelt wheat chaff left over after harvesting was used to temper clay for the pottery (briquetage) needed for the production, transport and storage of salt; similar chaff-tempered pottery has been found all over Britain.

By the end of the Roman occupation of Britain, the countryside would have changed radically. The square fields of the Iron Age were gradually replaced by larger, rectangular fields which were more suitable to the improved ploughs of the Roman period. The presence of the military and the development of towns would have led to previously farmed land being covered with buildings full of people who required food, while the introduction of new techniques and tools meant that areas of the country would have been brought into cultivation for the first time. The provision of well-maintained roads and bridges would have given farmers hitherto unknown access to new markets where they could sell their produce and thus the incentive to aim for higher yields. Even the rural architecture had changed from roundhouses accommodating single, if extended families, to extensive groupings of rectangular buildings housing owners, farmhands, animals and produce separately. The countryside of Britain would never be quite the same again.

Chapter 5
Domestic Life

As was discussed in earlier chapters, archaeologists have striven for many years to identify the use to which each room in a Romano-British house was put, with varying degrees of success, as the arrangements inside a house, whether it was in the town or country, would have depended largely on the origins and traditions of its occupants. It is likely that some families, if they came from the Eastern provinces, divided their accommodation into women's and men's quarters, while others had public and private spaces and/or rooms reserved for the use of family and servants. These divisions are not always easy to discern archaeologically. Some rooms, such as those in a bathsuite or an apsed dining room, are usually obvious because of their underfloor heating system and room shapes, but it has rarely proved possible to be sure which spaces were intended as bedrooms or sitting rooms.

In the most basic homes, there may have been little differentiation between the rooms. In the aisled farmhouses, as we have seen, the lack of substantial divisions within the earliest buildings suggests that there was little privacy, and it would appear that different generations of a family, together with their workforce and probably their livestock, occupied the same space. This arrangement would have been familiar to those who had lived or continued to live in a roundhouse, where activities were focussed around a central hearth. Various areas within the roundhouse may have been recognised as work areas, sleeping areas or public areas, but physical barriers between these spaces may have been quite ephemeral or have relied simply on an understanding within the family as to what happened where, and this may have varied from family to family.

Interior decoration

In the houses built along Roman lines, the evidence of the interior decoration often indicates which rooms were on public display and which were not. Mosaics, made up of small squares of coloured tile or stone set into a matrix, first appear in domestic buildings in Britain around

AD 75–80 and quickly became popular, to the extent that quite simple wattle-and-daub town houses in Colchester and Verulamium and villas at Eccles and Rivenhall had at least one mosaic floor before the end of the first century AD. These were usually in the first room reached from the front door, which was the room used for visitors. The larger houses had mosaics in all their principle rooms and along their main corridors, although it is noticeable that the more elaborate patterns are confined to the rooms used for entertaining and the designs become plainer or peter out completely as they merge into the areas used purely by the family or their servants.

By using mosaic, it was possible to make elaborately decorated floors which would cover uneven surfaces, be resistant to damp, were easily repaired and were hard-wearing. As a result, it is rare to find replacement floors, most households being content to keep the floors laid down by their predecessors. The earliest mosaics had black-and-white or red-and-white geometric patterns with simple, repetitive motifs; an example from Silchester, AD 140–160, with an all-over meander pattern incorporating other motifs in scattered squares, shows how effective these could be. By the end of the second century, however, figured panels began to appear in the wealthier homes with mythological scenes being especially popular.

Less elaborate flooring made from *opus sectile*, where stones cut into geometric shapes were laid in attractive patterns, was also popular, while at Piddington Villa, there was a floor with a herringbone motif of yellow and red tiles. In bathhouses, and other areas where waterproof surfaces were required, *opus signinum* made from crushed tiles mixed with mortar was effective. Wooden floors were installed in town houses in Colchester and Leicester, particularly in houses with cellars, but in the poorer dwellings, beaten earth would have sufficed.

Stone, particularly imported marble, was not only confined to the floors but also used to decorate the walls. The houses of London, for example, have revealed wall veneers of Purbeck marble, Rutland and Oxfordshire oolites and Collyweston slate as well as a range of coloured stones acquired from all over the Roman Empire. Most people, however, preferred their exterior and interior house walls plastered and painted. The outer walls were usually monochrome but might have thin red lines to give the impression of ashlar blocks. The most common fashion for the interior walls was to divide them into three horizontal panels. The lower might be painted to represent marble or wooden panels; at Sparsholt, the double band of *guilloches* on the floor is cunningly repeated on the wall to make the room look bigger. The upper register was usually plain, with deep red being the most popular colour. Elaborate decoration was reserved for the middle panel and by the mid-second century might have included architectural motifs, giving a *trompe l'oeil* effect of columns and arches or a peep into imaginary further rooms. In the third and fourth centuries, more elaborate scenes involving figures were common in the larger establishments.

Wall paintings can be found all over the province, from military buildings on Hadrian's Wall to villas on the Isle of Wight. They can be found in town houses, shops and public buildings, as well as in rural villas of varying degrees of sophistication. Like mosaics, wall paintings could be used as status symbols, reflecting the financial standing, elegant taste or level of education of their owners and, as such, could be used to project a family's image of themselves to the rest of the world. At Iwerne Minster (Dorset), the family may have had minimal funds or a limited social life as even in the fourth century the villa only had one room with painted walls, while the villa owners at Winterton (Lincolnshire), from the evidence of the wall decoration in 11 of its 16 rooms, seem to have had more public commitments. It is noticeable that in the larger houses, the quality of the wall paintings was subject to a sliding scale of magnificence, with the most artistic endeavours confined to the walls of the main public rooms, while the less public rooms had a correspondingly less impressive level of decoration. Even in the most expensive homes, however, few walls show more than one layer of paint, suggesting that it was a rare household that regularly gave their home a 'makeover'.

To modern eyes, the décor of a Romano-British room would appear too busy, with little attempt to match the floor mosaics with the treatment of the walls. In the case of the ceilings, this lack of co-ordination is also noticeable. Ceilings usually had a coat of plain white paint, which might have coloured rosettes, as at Fishbourne, but some decorators used painted stylised garlands to divide the ceiling into smaller compartments; in other rooms, paint was applied in imitation of the Italian fashion of coffering. In bathhouses, the blue-green background of the walls could be extended onto the ceiling, complete with images of fish and other sea creatures, to give the bathers an impression of being under water.

The owner of the bathhouse at Gorhambury took this underwater theme a stage further by glazing the windows with blue glass. Not all house windows were glazed; some were simply shuttered and barred. Those that did have glass would have been less draughty but would still have had limited light as windows were often high up, near the roof line. Pouring molten glass into sanded moulds to produce the panes invariably resulted in a very pale green glass of varying thickness, which was translucent rather than transparent. Despite the fact that many villas were built where there was a good view, few residents would have been able to see this view from the comfort of their living rooms.

The translucency of the glass, and the use of dark colours on the walls and floors, meant that artificial lighting was essential and this was provided by oil lamps, candles and torches. The lamps were made of pottery, iron or bronze and had a central well to hold the fuel, spouts to take a wick and a handle to allow the lamp to be carried or held safely for filling. The amount of light given out would have depended on the number of wicks. Oil lamps require constant maintenance, either trimming the wicks to avoid smuts or refilling the small reservoirs with olive oil: a tablespoonful of oil will only burn for about two hours. In the mid-second century, oil lamps seem to have largely disappeared from use in Britain, and the inhabitants had to rely more on candles made of wax or tallow – rendered animal fat. There are a number of references to the acquisition of tallow in the Vindolanda writing tablets, and in Letter 184, we learn that it was bought in 2 *denarii* amounts. Candlesticks for single candles, as well as multi-branched candelabra, have been found, but many people may have simply stuck their candles onto the nearest flat surface with molten wax.

In the roundhouses, windows, and thus window glass, were not included; lighting the interior and letting in air was achieved by opening the door. If the residents wished to keep the house warm, the door had to be kept shut so that they could derive some benefit from the central hearth, which was used for both heating and cooking. In the town houses and villas, tiled open hearths were placed in the centre of some rooms and others had fireplaces set into the walls, but some rooms in the new houses were heated by hypocausts. This required the floors to be raised on short pillars to allow hot air from an outside stokehole to circulate. Connecting hollow tiles, built into the walls, carried fumes up to air vents while providing all round heat. This was an efficient method but relied on access to fuel and reliable personnel, as someone had to be available to keep the fires going. Like modern solid fuel systems, it was more economical if the fires were kept at a constant temperature, rather than allowing the rooms to cool down and having to restart the system each day. Many homes, however, only had a hypocaust system in their public rooms, suggesting that most families normally relied on braziers and only fired up the hypocaust when visitors were expected.

Furniture

The comfort of a room would rely on its furnishings, little of which survives from Roman Britain, but scenes on tombstones, mostly from the military areas, give some indication of the type of furniture to be found in many homes. On the tombstone of Julia Velva from York, for example, the deceased woman lies on a bed with a substantial mattress and carved ends (see Illustration 17). By the bedhead, the man who paid for the memorial, Aurelius Mercurialis, stands in front of a wooden chair with clawed feet while a woman sits at the foot of the bed in a basket chair; in the centre, a smaller figure stands ready to pour wine from a jug into vessels laid out on a three-legged table of the sort which is known to have been made in wood, stone and Kimmeridge shale. A similar table can be seen in front of the couch on which Julia Velva's neighbours, Aelia Aeliana and her husband, recline, while Regina from South Shields sits on a large basket chair with a cushion to make it more comfortable (see Illustration 1). By Regina's side, there is a two-handled basket holding balls of wool; both chair and basket remind us that most households would have relied heavily on basketry for furnishings and containers, but little survives in the archaeological record.

Folding iron stools, of the type found at Bartlow Hills and Holborough, may have been more common than the surviving evidence might imply. Like the basket chairs, these would have been very uncomfortable without cushions of fabric or leather, stuffed with straw, hay or chaff; it is also possible that the hair referred to in a Vindolanda writing tablet was intended for stuffing cushions or mattresses (*Tab. Vindol.* 596).

Images on tombstones, such as that of Victor at South Shields (see Illustration 13), or fragments found in excavations, point to cushions being decorated with tassels, embroidered strips and appliqué. A purple wool cushion from Colchester was decorated with gold ribbon. Other soft furnishings mentioned in the Vindolanda tablets are towels, bedspreads, coverlets and curtains of various colours. Fragments of material found on Roman sites are usually presumed to be from clothing, but these references indicate a range of drapery that rarely survives. It is always possible that if a household disliked the mosaic floors or painted walls inherited from their predecessors, they could cover them with rugs or curtains, rather than go to the expense and disruption of having them replaced.

The more basic furniture would have been made of wood. Solid tables would have been regularly used in kitchens but have not yet been recognised in the fragments of wood found in excavations. In the villas of the south-west of Britain, stone tables or sideboards do survive, with geometric motifs carved along the front edge and the back edge butting up against a wall or set into a niche. These were supported on carved legs or brackets. Built-in or free-standing cupboards must also have been common for the storage of food, clothes or equipment. At Chalk, Kent, a cupboard was built to take advantage of the space under the stairs.

Housework

The more complicated the furnishings in a house, the more demanding the housework would have been, if everything was to be kept in good order and presentable to visitors. In some houses, the local environment would have conspired against a high standard of cleanliness: at Cirencester, the houses in Insula XXIII were built with their porticos on a level with the roadside, with the result that as passing traffic ground the road surface down, the dust was washed into the houses. More forward-thinking householders considered the housework at the design stage: at Colliton Park, one dwelling had been carefully planned so that the floors of connecting rooms were progressively lowered; washing the floors was a simple matter of starting at the top and working down. Having a drain in the corner of a kitchen, as at Frocester (Gloucestershire), or in mosaic floors, would also have aided floor cleaning.

Cleaning equipment, such as brooms and mops, is not easy to identify, although fragments of a few scrubbing brushes and yard brooms have been found. Pieces of cloth for dusting and polishing are, of course, impossible to differentiate from fragments of clothing. Cedar oil, juniper oil and beeswax would have been used for polishing furniture, in particular the shale tables which required regular oiling to protect them from dying out and splitting. Metal tableware would also have required polishing; regular buffing with bare hands would have kept the plainer pieces shiny but embossed or incised plates and jugs would have required the use of water and vinegar solutions or chalk rubbed on with leather cloths.

Clothing and soft furnishings would have needed to be laundered. This is a topic which rarely provides archaeological evidence so it must be presumed that large bowls or buckets were used, unless a dwelling was close to a pond or stream. In the towns, a householder would have had access to fullers, who would wash clothes professionally as well as dress newly woven cloth. Laundry may have been thrown over a line or bushes or from trees to dry. Ironing by heat was not used, but there is some evidence that creases were erased by rubbing the cloth with glass smoothers, a method that was still used in parts of Britain at the beginning of the twentieth century.

Clothing

Tombstones provide occasional glimpses of the clothing worn by the people of Roman Britain. The basic item of clothing for men, women and children, regardless of status, was the 'Gallic coat' (see Illustration 6). This was a tunic made from two rectangular pieces of woollen cloth for the body and two further rectangles sewn into position for the sleeves. The hems might be curved to avoid them sagging at the sides and they were worn to the knee by men and to the ankle or mid-calf by women. Men usually wore their tunics with a belt, but women preferred to leave their tunics free at the waist, only rarely using a tied girdle. Under the tunic, men, particularly those from Britain or one of the other north-west provinces, wore trousers. Under this, again, some men wore underpants, probably of linen, while women wore an undertunic, also of linen. Women may also have worn linen knickers; the examples made of leather which have been found at Shadwell, and elsewhere, were probably intended as costumes for entertainers and sportswomen rather than as daily underwear. There is some evidence that a simple linen band tied around the chest did service as a brassière for those women who required support. As an outer garment, both men and women would have worn cloaks of varying shapes and sizes; women are also depicted on their tombstones wearing shawls. A fringed herringbone twill hood, decorated with tablet-woven bands, found in Orkney, shows how these outer garments could be both elegant and efficient (Gabra-Sanders 2001).

On the whole, the garments worn by men varied little over the years nor did their style depend much on the wearer's origins. The clothing of women, on the other hand, often reflects their tribal traditions more than the whims of fashion. An outfit consisting of a close-fitting bodice with long, tight sleeves with cuffs, and covered by a loose tunic in the form of a tube with the back and front held together with brooches at the shoulder, was popular at the end of the Iron Age and in the early Roman period in Britain and the German provinces. This is usually referred to as Menimane's costume, after the widow of Blussus who appears on her husband's tombstone at Mainz Weisenau in Germany (Wild 1968). The women of the *Ubii* tribe from Eastern Europe wore a series of tunics, one on top of the other, with a voluminous cloak and a very large bonnet which enclosed all their hair. Women from the Mediterranean countries, such as Julia Pacata in London and the senator's daughter Julia Lucilla at High Rochester, may have continued to wear the sleeveless or short-sleeved tunic known as the *stola*, although this seems to have gone out of fashion in Rome by the late first century AD and would have been an inadequate garment in which to face a British winter.

Tribal origins may also have prescribed whether a woman wore a headdress or not as there is little evidence that covering the head was related to a particular stage in a woman's life, except among the women from Noricum and Pannonia. Besides the *Ubii*, women from the Treveri tribe in Gaul wore a close-fitting cap of fine linen; similar bonnets can be seen worn by the two women on Julia Velva's tombstone (see Illustration 17) and on a sculptured head from Birrens in Scotland. The fabric found covering the head of a child's skeleton at Holborough was made of silk woven in geometric damask with different colours giving a small check pattern. In the fourth century, wearing a veil became more common as women followed the lead of the empresses.

Analysis of fragments of cloth found in excavations and the evidence of wall paintings and mosaics indicate that both men and women in Roman Britain enjoyed wearing bright colours. Purple cloth has been found at York, russet brown at Caerwent, red at Vindolanda, black and grey at London and even a tartan of yellow and brown at Falkirk, indicating that the population was utilising all the natural dyestuffs that could be found in the country, such as woad which would have provided both blue and black dye. The red dye used at Vindolanda has been shown by analysis to have been derived from the local bedstraw, rather than madder from Gaul, while lichen found in the neighbourhood also produces a clear purple similar to that obtained from the more expensive, imported orchil.

A surprising range of weaves has been identified among the fabrics found: two-over-two diamond and herringbone twills, two-over-two weave with chevron patterns and half-basket weaves have been found, supplementing the more basic weaves. Using different weaves would have introduced individuality and texture into clothing. Tablet-woven or heddle-woven patterned bands would also be sewn to garments to make them more attractive.

Shoes worn in Britain before the Roman invasion were made from single sheets of hide, tied on with leather thongs. These varied markedly, depending on the region in which they were made and worn, and were used by men and women of all ages. Some had openwork designs cut through their uppers to contrast with the stockings or socks worn underneath. Single-piece shoes reflecting Roman fashions begin to appear in the province at a very early date, not always to the benefit of the wearers – the appearance of bunions on the feet of skeletons seems to coincide with the introduction of the new types of footwear.

Both men and women wore outdoor boots made from coloured leather which covered the entire foot. Those found in London either have openwork uppers, suggesting that they were not worn by labourers, or are plain ankle boots. The latter are seamed at the front and thonged at the instep. An example of the former, found in a burial at Southfleet (Kent), was of gilded purple leather and shows the late-second- to early-third-century development to openwork embellished with embroidery or gilding. After AD 130, this type of footwear was largely replaced by the latchet shoe, which had a round toe and a strap across the instep.

The wearing of the military boot, or *caliga*, was probably confined to men, but an equally substantial boot was worn by civilians in the third century. This had a front fastening and integrally cut laces. The hobnails on the underside of the sole were often arranged in patterns, but nailed shoes were no longer fashionable by the end of the fourth century; at Lankhills cemetery, the indications are that women and children had abandoned the style before the men.

Sandals were initially worn by only women and children, with the soles following the line of the foot, but in the third century, women's

sandals became narrower. Men adopted the style in the late second
century, but the changes in fashion dictated that their sandals became
rounder and blunter in shape, until they were practically triangular.
It is likely that sandals were only worn out of doors in the summer.
Men tended to regard them as house shoes, and it was considered polite
to remove them when reclining to dine formally. The soles of the early
sandals consisted of several layers of leather stitched together and with
a single row of nails around the edge. The principle thong usually
started between the big toe and the second toe. Slippers were worn only
by women, although examples with thick wooden or cork soles may
have been used by both sexes to protect their feet from hot floors in the
bathhouse.

A range of accessories has been found. Sculpture shows women
carrying bags of various shapes, some clearly made of leather but others
are more like a 'Dorothy bag' and were probably made of cloth with
a draw string. A purse made of leather with a linen lining was found
in a barrow at Holborough. A container of bronze, with a lid secured
by a clip and an expanding strip handle, like a bracelet, was clearly
designed to be worn on the upper arm; discoveries of these purses are
confined to the military zones and may have been army issue. Fans and
parasols made from ivory or bone have been found at York. An example
of a fan, showing how they unfurl to form a circle on a handle, can
be seen on a tombstone from Murrell Hill in Carlisle. Examples found
elsewhere in the empire suggest that the fabric between the spokes could
be cloth or chicken skin.

Jewellery

The most common accessories found are pieces of jewellery. Large neck
rings, known as torcs, had been worn in Iron Age Britain and carried
magico-religious significance as well as indications of status. Torcs were
also awarded to Roman soldiers as rewards for valour, but after the first
century AD, both sexes began to wear them as symbols of good luck.
More delicate necklaces made of metal chains or strung beads were
mostly worn by women, although there is evidence emerging that
the priests of certain religious sects, such as the *gallus* from Catterick
(*Cataractonium*), also affected beaded necklaces. Finds from graves
indicate that women might wear several bracelets on each arm, although

one bracelet on each wrist was more common, as can be seen on Regina's tombstone (see Illustration 1). Bracelets, like necklaces, could be made from beads of glass, jet and semi-precious stones – pearls, amber, coral and emeralds were popular – but could also be made from single pieces of glass, shale, metal or bone, the latter fashioned from strips steamed to make them flexible enough to bend and be held in position with metal collars. Anklets have also been found.

Earrings were more usually worn by women but always designed for a pierced ear. The most common type is a plain penannular ring of metal that could be easily slipped on or off, but other examples have twisted ends, implying that they were inserted and then left *in situ*. Pendants of semi-precious stones or glass could be hung from these earrings. Other, more expensive, examples had semi-precious stones incorporated into their design.

Finger rings were worn by both sexes, either as decoration or to carry intaglios which were used for sealing documents. Rings were regularly given as gifts, often carrying encouraging mottos, and the frequent mention of lost or stolen rings in the Bath curse tablets suggests that many had sentimental value for their owners. Rings might be exchanged between couples on betrothal or marriage; a practice from the Eastern provinces was for an iron ring to be placed on the third finger of a woman's left hand by her fiancé as part of the betrothal ceremony. In the north-west provinces, however, an iron ring was regarded as a symbol of slavery. The gold open-work ring, found at Corbridge, which carries the motto Aemilia Zeses (Aemilia may you live), may have been used as a betrothal ring (see Illustration 14) as may the many examples of rings bearing clasped hands motifs.

Brooches rarely appear in matching sets of jewellery as these, however decorative, were largely seen as fastenings for clothing. The brooches with a marked curve to their bows were particularly used to fasten cloaks, but brooches chained together in pairs would have been essential elements of women's clothing in their early centuries of Roman rule as they were used to pin the tunics into position (see Illustration 15). Small plate brooches in the shape of animals or shoes, however, would not have confined much cloth efficiently and may well have been worn to denote membership of a guild or religious cult and used more as a badge than a brooch. Most brooches are made of bronze, sometimes gilded or silvered to copy the more expensive examples of gold or silver. Enamelling was used to add colour to both bow and plate brooches.

Personal grooming

Although there is limited evidence for fashion in clothing, the many changes in hairstyles imply that both men and women sought to look up to date whenever possible. In the Iron Age, most British women had worn their hair loose or in bunches or a plait, and it was only in the first century that the hairpin became common in the province, allowing women to wear their hair in a simple bun at the back of the neck; this style probably never died out in the rural areas but made a reappearance in the towns as a result of the influence of Christianity. Those women with social pretensions, however, would have looked carefully at the latest coins issued by empresses, as the empress of the time was considered to be the leader of fashion throughout the empire. This becomes evident in the Flavian period when the complicated hairstyles of the Italian aristocracy can be seen on Romano-British sculpture. Later on, the visit of Julia Domna, wife of Septimius Severus, to Britain led many women to adopt the Syrian style, in which the hair hangs in crimped waves down the sides of the face before being taken up the back of the head in a large roll interlaced with ribbons.

Men were not immune to the vagaries of fashion. The beard affected by the Emperor Hadrian led to many men giving up shaving, while imperial haircuts can also be seen on provincial men, usually a few years after they were fashionable in Italy. Both men and women would have used bone combs to get the effect they sought; evidence for the curling tongs mentioned in classical literature has not been found, but some styles would have demanded their use. Rectangular or circular sheets of polished metal, held in wooden frames or in the lids of toilet boxes, were the most common mirrors, but larger metal discs, with either handles protruding from one edge or across the back, were also used. Examples of glass mirrors, imported from Germany, have been found at Reculver (*Regulbium*), York and Ospringe (Kent). These were silvered on the back but are very small and would only have been suitable for applying eye make-up. No mirror larger than a modern dinner plate has been found so far in the province, and it is unlikely that anyone in Roman Britain ever saw what they looked like full length or even very clearly.

Literary evidence tells us that both men and women resorted to cosmetics to improve upon nature. The analysis of the contents of a small tin box, found in London, has revealed a fat-based ointment that may have been intended as a face cream or foundation. The discovery of other

1. Tombstone of Regina from South Shields.

2. Iron Age grave group from Welwyn.

3. The entrance to the strongroom in the Headquarters Building at Chesters Roman fort.

4. Shield boss with its owner's name along one edge. Found in the River Tyne.

5. Prestwick Carr Hoard of paterae and cauldrons.

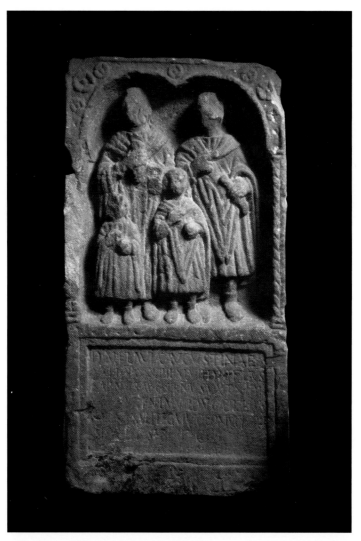

6. Tombstone of Flavia Augustina from York.

7. Tomb of Volusia Faustina from Lincoln.

8. Tombstone of a smith god from York.

9. Sestertius of Hadrian from the River Tyne at Newcastle upon Tyne.

10. The Verulamium amphitheatre.

11. Aerial photograph of Romano-British settlement site.

12. Wallpainting showing the portrait of a young woman, Sparsholt.

13. Tombstone of Victor from South Shields.

14. Finger ring of Aemilia from Corbridge.

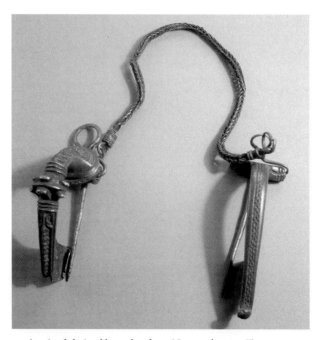

15. A pair of chained brooches from Newcastle upon Tyne.

16. Cooking pot repaired with a lead clamp from South Shields.

17. Tombstone of Julia Velva from York.

18. Altar to Antenociticus from Benwell showing focus, mouldings and knife.

19. Reconstruction of Carrawburgh Mithraeum.

20. Figurine of a priestess from South Shields.

21. Lullingstone 'orantes' wall painting.

22. Page from the *Notitia Dignitatum*.

containers and long-handled scoops, known as *ligulae*, indicates that cosmetics and perfumes were commonly used, although it is not always possible to say which were used for cosmetics and which had a medical purpose. Small bronze, boat-shaped objects have been identified as grinders for mineral-based cosmetics, while a fragment of a glass vessel in the form of a bird, from Silchester, is of a type used in the first century AD for exporting face powder from Northern Italy.

Perfumes were used extensively. Country dwellers may have made scents from wild or cultivated plants for their own use or for sale, but there was also a market for imported perfumes and scented oils which were bought in small glass flasks called *unguentaria*. Some of these flasks resemble modern test tubes, but a ring-shaped vessel has been found at York and a very long container with a jet lid and 'dip-stick' was found in the famous Spitalfields woman's burial in London. One vessel from York has the word Patrimoni on its base, which is probably the name of the manufacturer. Glass *unguentaria* are mostly of pale green glass, similar to window glass, but brightly coloured versions are also known. At Catterick, a very elegant bronze perfume flask, decorated with red- and blue-enamelled motifs, and still with its lid in place, had been relegated to a glue pot at some time in its life.

Tweezers were used by both sexes to remove unwanted hair as well as splinters in the fingers. Tweezers are often found as elements in small hygiene sets, known as chatelaines, in which a ring or bar holds several tools, such as toothpicks and ear-scoops. There is literary evidence that both men and women in polite Roman society removed hair from their legs and from under their arms, but it is not possible to say how far this was practiced in Britain (Ovid *Ars Amatoria* III.197, I.505–506; Pliny *Naturalis Historia* XXVIII.249, 255).

Kitchens

An essential part of any house is the kitchen, but this room can be surprisingly difficult to identify in a Roman house. In the roundhouses, food would have been cooked on the central, kerbed hearth and would have been confined to whatever could be produced using a spit, cauldron or pot. In those town houses and villas with multiple rooms, one was usually set aside for preparing and cooking food. At Newport Villa, the kitchen was next to a bathsuite, possibly to take advantage of the supply of hot water as the tiled hearth was built up against the party wall. The villa at Spoonley Wood had the equivalent of a modern fitted kitchen with a stone floor, stone-lined well and two stone table supports.

It was not essential in a Romano-British kitchen to have a built-in hearth. Most cooking was done over charcoal, and this could be carried out using tripods and gridirons. A reconstruction at the Museum of London shows a gridiron being used on a tile-and-clay platform with a charcoal storage space underneath. Gridirons could also be used on a fire built on a large tile or stone set into a bench or the floor. The use of charcoal as a cooking fuel would have had its dangers, and excavations, as at Greta Bridge in County Durham, have shown that several homes were destroyed by fires which started in the kitchen. Some householders considered it prudent to isolate the cooking completely from the main house: a thatched building at Lullingstone Villa has been interpreted as a separate cookhouse.

Town dwellers might have had the luxury of buying their bread from a baker, but in the country, home baking would have been essential. A household at Bourton-on-the-Water (Gloucestershire) had a bread oven built in the third century. This consisted of an oval domed structure, built out of the local stone, with a narrow mouth and a clay floor. A fire would be lit inside and allowed to burn until the requisite temperature was reached; the ashes were then raked out, the bread dough placed inside and the door sealed. In the winter, it may well have been difficult to reach and maintain a high enough temperature to make good bread.

Kitchens would not have been pleasant places to work. Window glass is rarely found in these domestic quarters, so light and air would have been available only by opening the wooden shutters. If the windows were kept closed to conserve heat, cooking with charcoal in a confined, poorly aired space would have resulted in a fuggy, smut-filled atmosphere. Nor were all householders particularly tidy: at Folkestone, a building had two kitchens, both of which had food debris and broken pottery strewn across the floor, jammed down behind the corner hearth and in an internal rubbish pit. Only the most expensive houses had water supplied direct to their kitchens, and most people would have needed to carry their daily water supplies from a nearby well, cistern or stream which would have limited their standards of kitchen hygiene. The lack of decent storage facilities also meant that meat and vegetables would need to be hung up to dry from the rafters, with the danger that they might rot. Using barrels or large pottery vessels in a damp, warm room would have resulted in the stored grain developing fungal spores, and this would have caused ergotism, which in turn can lead to convulsions, hallucinations, gangrene and abortion (Roberts and Cox 2003, 195). Excavations of latrines and drains have shown that the inhabitants of Roman Britain were riddled with intestinal worms as a result of poor hygiene.

By the second century AD, a British kitchen would have looked very different to the cooking area in a roundhouse. Having the cooking surface raised up meant that cooks no longer had to squat over the fire, as had been required with a central hearth. There would also be a number of pieces of kitchen equipment that were new. Most small households would have continued to use the 'beehive' quern, with its domed upper stone, to grind their corn, but in the larger homes, the more efficient, flat rotary quern of the military, with its handle fixed to the side of the upper stone by an iron band, would have become popular. Some large villas had mills powered by donkeys and even water mills.

Most recipes required some or all of their ingredients to be pulverised. Pottery bowls with gritted inner surfaces, known as mortaria, have been identified as vessels designed for the task as most have pouring lips, so that their contents could be transferred to a cooking pot, and deep overhanging lips to hold them firmly in iron stands while their contents were being pulped by a stone pestle. Initially, all mortaria were imported from the Continent, but British potteries soon started to offer local products and large numbers have been found on Britain sites. Hilary Cool (2006), however, has recently pointed out that not all mortaria may have been used in the kitchen and, when they were, may not necessarily have been used to follow Roman recipes in the Roman manner.

Pottery used for storing and cooking food came in a range of sizes from vast grain bins to tiny spice pots. Lids could be purposely made from pottery or wood but were often simple discs cut from broken pots or pieces of stone. Flagons were usually pale buff in colour, while the jugs, dishes and bowls were invariably red or grey. Although archaeologists delight in analysing food residues from unglazed pottery, it is salutary to realise that the presence of these residues is an indicator of how difficult it was to keep earthenware clean and those fabrics with large inclusions of shell or grit must have become unpleasantly unhygienic quite quickly. There were many sources from which new pots could be bought, so the fact that many are found with breaks roughly repaired with lead clamps may indicate that not everyone could afford to replace their broken crockery (see Illustration 16).

Because it was easier to clean, bronze would have been preferred to pottery if affordable. Soldiers were issued with bronze saucepans, which we today refer to as *paterae*, and they were also used in civilian kitchens. A hoard of paterae and cauldrons, all heavily and inexpertly patched until they could no longer be used, was found at Prestwick Carr in Northumberland (Plate 5). A Vindolanda letter tells us that in the first century AD each patera could cost up to 5 *denarii*, so it is hardly surprising that Oceana at Bath felt obliged to seek divine intervention when one of her pans was stolen (*Tab. Sul.* 60).

Colanders of bronze may not have been used for straining vegetables but for warming or cooling wine by placing hot coals or ice in them and pouring the wine over to drain into a bowl beneath. That paterae and colander handles are both flat and echo each other's shape has been taken as evidence that they could be used as sets for serving wine. Pottery colanders may have had a more prosaic use, although a pottery funnel with a built-in strainer, found at Richborough (*Rutupiae*), would have been a very useful piece of equipment. Small pots with concentric ribs around their perforated bases are thought to have been used as cheese presses.

Frying pans of iron, with folding handles, or, less commonly, of bronze have been found. At Housesteads, a flat iron disc on a long handle has been identified as a baker's peel, a handy gadget used for taking loaves out of a hot oven. Lead was also used, particularly for reducing wine, and the analysis of human bones at Poundbury in Dorset has shown that this resulted in people ingesting significant amounts of lead.

Glass was rarely used in the kitchen, except for storing liquids. Mould blown, square or cylindrical bottles, capable of holding a quarter to half a litre, are common finds and often the only glass vessels to emerge from rural sites. Contents analysis shows that they invariably held olive oil, but their robustness meant that they were reused for a variety of purposes, even as cinerary urns. Their handles are flattened so that they do not project beyond their walls and so could be packed into crates for transit.

Diet

The Vindolanda writing tablets give a fascinating insight into what was being eaten in a military milieu, and archaeological evidence indicates that people living in towns and villas had a similar diet, albeit with some regional differences and constrained by a family's income. As today, the daily diet divides into the day-to-day basics, such as cereals or meat; the more interesting items that give food flavour, such as leeks, onions and pepper; and the special items that come under the heading of occasional treats. Some of these, such as the meat, leave obvious traces in the animal bone assemblages.

The quantity of animal bones found in excavations shows that a large amount of meat was consumed, including lamb and mutton, veal and beef, boar, pig and goat. Red, roe and fallow deer were also eaten, although they did not form a staple to the diet. Butchery marks have also been found on frogs' legs, as well as on the bones of horses, hares, dogs and even elk. Cow bones are often found broken in order for the marrow to be extracted.

Chicken bones occur in most excavation assemblages, and ducks and geese were eaten, as well as a wide range of wild birds, most of whom we would not consider edible today, such as coot, avocet, water rail and golden plover. Some, such as cranes and the great bustard, are no longer native to Britain. To supplement the diet, doves were kept in *columbaria*, and Barnsley Park has produced evidence that pheasants may have been hand-reared. The eggs of domestic fowl were essential to the diet and the scale of consumption can be deduced from Letter 302 at Vindolanda when the writer orders 'a hundred or two hundred eggs if they are for sale there at a fair price'. To ensure a supply of eggs when the hens were not laying, eggs could be preserved by soaking them in olive oil or by rubbing them with salt and packing them in bran or chaff. The eggs of wild birds, particularly sea birds, were considered a delicacy.

The nearer to a river or the sea someone lived, the more likely they were to include fish in their diet, but there must have been an efficient system for transporting sea fish to inland customers as Silchester has produced grey mullet and herring bones in its assemblages, sea bream has been found at Uley, and, in Wiltshire, there is evidence for flounders, bass, herring and horse mackerel at Great Bedwyn. River and pond fish were also caught, including pike, which was eaten by the native British but does not appear to have been favoured by incomers from the Mediterranean. At Shakenoak, the discovery of three fish ponds suggests that villa owners bred coarse fish for the table. Those with more exotic tastes might import tunny fish in oil from Provence or North Africa; an amphora fragment from Carlisle records that it held 'Old Tangiers tunny relish, "provisions" quality, excellent quality' (Tomlin 2003b, 176).

Shellfish were popular throughout the country and would have been regularly traded from the coast to inland towns and villas. Among the more familiar crabs, cockles, periwinkles, scallops and whelks, more unusual shellfish, such as prickly cockle, otter shell and peppery furrow shell, have been found in domestic contexts. Several sites have produced evidence for the eating of the edible snail (*Helix aspersa*) and the escargot (*Helix pomatia*). Just about every Roman site in Britain has produced oyster shells, and these would have had to be transported quickly and carefully, covered in sea water in barrels with tarred inner surfaces, but traces of these barrels have not been found. A properly made barrel, of course, is easily recycled, and some would have made the trip many times before being reduced to that invariable fate of a good barrel: being used as a well lining.

Through writers such as Pliny and the compilation of recipes attributed to Apicius, we know a great deal about how the Romans cooked their food. One vital ingredient was known as *garum* or *liquamen*. This was a sauce made from the salted, fermented entrails of large fish and small complete fish. The resulting liquid was used as a condiment. Most fish sauce was imported into Britain from Italy, Libya or Spain, although some came from France as is attested from an inscribed amphora from Southwark which advertises 'Lucius Tettius Africanus's finest fish sauce from Antipolis' (Antibes). Such was the demand that a British fish-sauce factory was established at the Peninsular House site on the Thames in London.

Several vegetable recipes include garum to give flavour, and lettuces, endive and cucumber, which today we would use raw in salads, were often braised. Beans, peas and other pulses could be dried and stored, but most vegetables were available only in their natural season, which would mean that they were either unobtainable or there was a glut. Root vegetables, such as the newly introduced radishes, white carrots, parsnips and turnips, could be stored for some months but were always at risk from mice or insects if they were not properly packed. Pollen and seed evidence suggests that nettles, Good King Henry, dandelion, sorrel and other wild herbs provided important sources of vitamins.

Many types of soft and tree fruit were already growing in Britain before the first century AD. Plums, apples, pears, strawberries, raspberries, elderberries and gooseberries were all eaten, although it is rarely clear if the fruit came from cultivated plants or the hedgerows. Fruit was eaten raw or in stews, and autumn must have been a busy time as fruit was gathered and bottled or pickled in vinegar. This would also have been the time when wild hedgerow berries, such as hips, haws, bullace and sloes, as well as hazelnuts and walnuts, were picked.

It should not be imagined that all the cooking was plain and basic. There is pottery evidence, mostly from military sites, that incomers from Africa and the Continent brought with them their culinary tastes and cooking methods and people seem to have been eager to try new recipes and sample the new imports of fruit and vegetables. British sites have produced evidence for the use of coriander, rue, savory, borage, fennel and mint, as well as the seeds of celery, dill and poppy. Three types of pepper were imported, and an elaborate gilded silver pepper grinder found at Hoxne indicates what a valued condiment this was. These herbs and spices were used in medicines as well as in cooking.

Olive oil quickly changed from an exotic import to an essential in the home, where it was used for lighting, medicine and lubrication as well as cooking. In the south of Britain, most olive oil came from Baetica in Southern Spain, but by the third century, the products of the North African olive groves started to dominate the trade. A complete amphora found in a shipwreck off the Pan Sands near Kent was still full of whole olives, indicating that the British had also developed a taste for eating the fruit as well as using the oil.

There is plenty of evidence that wine were transported around the empire in amphorae but could also be moved by barrel. From the literary sources and from the amphorae, we know that this alcohol came in a range of qualities, from the very expensive from Gallia Narbonensis or Falernia to the cheapest *vin ordinaire*. In the Vindolanda writing tablets, there are references to lees of wine bought from Isuria for a quarter of a *denarius* (*Tab. Vindol.* 185); this refers to the dregs found at the bottom of a bottle or barrel, which was drunk diluted as a cheap drink. Beer could be brewed from barley or wheat in-house but was also transported some distances, as is shown by a letter from the decurion Mascelus to Flavius which states 'my fellow soldiers have no beer. Please order some to be sent' (*Tab. Vindol.* 62). This beer was carried and stored in barrels and measured both in *modii* and by *metretam*, which was equal to 100 *sextarii*. Remains of tankards show that beer was drunk in quarts, rather than pints. Both beer and wine were preferred to water, which might be tainted, or to milk, which, as was mentioned earlier, was regarded as suitable only for children and invalids.

How and when someone ate their meals would have revealed a great deal about them in Roman Britain. Those who worked in the fields or in industry probably had a basic breakfast of bread and water before setting out on their day. Their main meal, possibly their only other meal, would be taken once the light had started to fade and their day's work was completed. Those who had a more leisured lifestyle might have followed the Roman habit of having a light breakfast, followed by a simple lunch and then a hearty three-course dinner with several removes mid-afternoon.

Leisure

It was at dinner that households entertained guests, displayed their best tableware and drank their most expensive wine. It was in the dining room that glass was used in the form of jugs, bowls, drinking beakers and plates; mostly imported in various colours from the Continent. Glass is a material that lends itself to a range of decorative techniques and tableware has been found with moulded, painted, engraved and faceted decoration. The best crockery would have included shiny red Samian from Gaul as well as pots with mica dusting, colour coating, rouletting and barbotine decoration. A few pots even had green glazed surfaces. It should not be supposed, however, that these pots represented the highest level of tableware; really wealthy households would have used silver, gilded bronze and even gold vessels when entertaining guests and such pieces were often given as presents, complete with engraved messages. From the second century, pewter plates, spoons, canisters, bowls and cups were considered acceptable gifts; one dish from Verulamium had the name of its owner, Viventia, scratched on its base as well as a number indicating that it was part of a set (*RIB* 2414.1).

A grave at Winchester included a typical place setting, consisting of a Samian cup and plate, two knives and a spoon, laid out on a shale tray. Forks were not used; etiquette demanded that food was to be first cut up with a knife and then eaten with the fingers. It was considered polite for guests to bring their own knife and spoon with them to functions and several could be folded to make them easier to carry. Again there are several examples with their owners' names or good luck messages scratched on to make them more personalised gifts.

There were several occasions when presents were exchanged. Betrothals, weddings and birthdays were all celebrated in this way, as were certain religious festivals such as the Saturnalia in December. It was also at these events that people would throw parties or invite friends round for dinner. At Vindolanda, Claudia Severa invited her friend Sulpicia Lepidina to her birthday party on the third day before the Ides of September (9 September) (*Tab. Vindol.* 244). Besides eating choice food and sipping the best wine, the hosts would be expected to entertain their guests by offering them a bath or by playing musical instruments. Surprisingly little is known about music in Roman Britain, and there are only a few instrument fragments and representations in art to give us any impression of the musical life of the inhabitants. These indicate that lyres, lutes and *citharae* were among the stringed instruments while the wind section included the tibia, a reed pipe which was played either singly or in pairs. An eight-pipe set of panpipes found at Shakenoak might be the *syrinx* described in Latin poetry; this is inscribed with the name Bellicia, presumably the owner. Simple single-note pipes of reed, bone, wood and clay have also been found.

A host might also suggest a stroll around the garden or, if the weather was favourable, have the meal outdoors. The Roman writer Diodorus Siculus was of the opinion that a garden was 'a useful device for avoiding confusion when crowds are present' (*Library of History* V.40) and many villas and town houses had a courtyard which could be used as an extra dining room. The large villa or palace at Fishbourne has revealed a formal arrangement of bedding trenches which may have held box hedging in a decorative parterre with occasional specimen trees. There is also evidence of a trellis for climbing plants, which was used as a screen for the entrance hall. Pollen evidence from Fishbourne, Frocester and other villas provides evidence for colourful gardens for much of the year using native plants, such as snowdrops, violets, daffodils, primroses and bluebells in the spring and oxeye daisies, irises, windflowers, forget-me-nots, foxgloves, marguerites and pinks in the summer. Pliny was scathing about the beauty of the native British roses, and it is possible that others, sharing his opinions, imported rose bushes from the Continent. At Alcester (*Alauna*), columbine and corn marigold have been found, which must have also been imported from the Eastern Mediterranean.

The existence of flower gardens shows that some British householders were wealthy enough to allow some of their land to be used for pleasure and were not concerned about using all of it for growing food and making a profit. Gardens also imply that some people had the time to supervise their gardeners or work on the flower beds themselves as well as the time and culture to enjoy the results.

Chapter 6
Religious Life

When studying the Roman Empire, the importance of religion for its inhabitants should not be underestimated. This is particularly true in the case of Roman Britain where religion played a part in every aspect of its inhabitants' lives. That said, most people took a somewhat pragmatic view of their relationship with their gods. Both native Britons and the incoming Romans were concerned with their own well-being and saw religion as a means to an end in ensuring that their lives were spent as prosperously and comfortably as possible. Very few deities were seen as having any particular connection with an afterlife; those that did, in religions such as Christianity and Mithraism, were very much in the minority.

The afterlife

The native population of Britain had always regarded the human soul as immortal and believed that there was a superior afterlife to which all people could aspire. At the beginning of the Roman period in Britain, however, most of the new inhabitants seem to have had severe doubts as to the existence of life after death. This attitude underwent a change around the Antonine period (AD 138–192), as can be seen by the provision of grave goods. Exactly what these burial artefacts were for is not always clear; few appear to follow the Pharaonic Egyptian model of attempting to provide the deceased with everything that might be needed in the next life. Many simply provide a picnic, an oil lamp and the stout shoes needed for the journey to the next world; others ensured that the mourners fully appreciated the status of the person being buried but were unlikely to be much use to the deceased themselves.

Several inscriptions offer insights into the different ideas people had of the afterlife. Dionysius Fortunatus, when mourning his mother, hoped that the earth would lie lightly upon her (*RIB* 1250), which may suggest that he thought the afterlife was near at hand. Graves which were linked to the ground surface by a pipe, so that liquid offerings could be provided on special feast days, also imply a belief that the dead stayed in close proximity (Toynbee 1971, 52). One translation of Flaminius Pansa's epitaph for his daughter at Risingham, on the other hand, portrays the afterlife as an unpleasant but more distant place where 'the ground is always frozen' (*RIB* 1253); Quintus Corellius Fortis, referring to 'Pluto's Acherusian realms' when 'bewailing' the 'final end' of his daughter, appears to have an equally gloomy impression of a remote next world (*RIB* 684). Symbols on other tombstones suggest more hopeful views: birds imply the concept of the flight of the soul heavenwards, while sea images, such as shells and dolphins, refer to the soul voyaging to the Islands of the Blessed. Coins found in some graves are likely to be the fare payable to Charon the Ferryman for safe passage across the river Styx.

There were several ways of disposing of the dead, from simple inhumations to cremation pyres with decorated byres and elaborate rites. These differences may be attributable to changes in fashion, as when inhumation became more popular from the second century AD onwards, but largely reflect the diverse origins of the inhabitants of Roman Britain. Burial rituals revealed through excavation show that the transient sections of the population, whether military or civilian, were particularly concerned that incorrect rituals did not hinder their progress to the next world. The recently published cemetery at Brougham, Cumbria, for example, shows that the population included people from Pannonia (the area of modern Hungary) who continued to practise the burial rituals of their native homelands (Cool 2004). Soldiers in the army expected part of their annual salary to be retained by the authorities to defray their funeral expenses should they die in service and often appointed a colleague as their heir to guarantee that there was a named individual with responsibility for ensuring that their body received the proper rites; in the case of Julius Valens at London, it was Flavius Attius who 'had the matter in charge' (*RIB* 13). Gaius Valerius, a standard-bearer in the Ninth Legion, left instructions in his will that a tombstone be set up in his memory when he died at Lincoln but appears not to have specified an executor (*RIB* 257). Others who were away from their families, such as merchants and slaves, joined burial clubs so that they could be confident that their bodies would be properly treated (see *RIB* 1620 at Housesteads). It is probable that this responsibility did not stop once the funeral was over; heirs and burial club members, like family members, may have been expected to visit the grave on set days, such as the feast of the Parentalia, and perform the traditional rituals.

In the first and second centuries, it was fashionable, particularly in military circles, to erect a tombstone in memory of a loved one. Some of these were very basic, simply recording the name of the deceased and possibly their age; others were more elaborate and recorded not only details of the dead person but also, through imagery, details of their appearance and lifestyle. The tombstones of Regina (see Illustration 1), Victor (see Illustration 13) and Julia Velva (see Illustration 17) offer a glimpse into the lives of those remembered in the inscriptions. Very few give any suggestion as to how someone died; Tadius Exuperatus whose memorial records his death 'on the German expedition' is a rare exception (*RIB* 369).

It was important to pay due reverence to the dead as there was an ever-present fear that, if they did not receive proper respect, they would return to harm the living. Most cemeteries had high surrounding walls or perimeter ditches to mark out the dividing line between the living and the dead, and it is possible that the practise of decapitation that is seen in many cemeteries in the south of Britain may have been intended to ensure that the dead stayed in their graves. Some bodies have been found lying on their faces with a heavy stone in the centre of their back, weighing them down, while stone tiles were arranged over the coffin of a child at Poundbury in Dorset. In the latter case, the fact that the child had been congenitally deaf may have led to this special treatment, as those with physical handicaps were regarded as particularly likely to haunt the living. At Brough-under-Stainmore, the Greek inscription on the tombstone of the sixteen-year-old Hermes of Commagene asks passing travellers to call out greetings to the child, reassuring them, 'nor will your words be false, for the lad was good, and you will do him a good service', in other words, the child did not deserve to return as a ghost and a cheery greeting would help him to avoid this fate (*RIB* 758).

Worship

During their lives, people might worship several deities. Everyone under Roman jurisdiction was expected to venerate the deities in the Roman pantheon, particularly Jupiter, Roma and the Deified Emperors, but many people also offered allegiance to the deities of their own homelands, as well as the more exotic deities introduced into the empire by travellers and the military. Individuals would have their favourite gods to whom they offered sacrifices on a regular basis; this might be seen as paying an insurance premium with health, wealth and happiness being the expected result. If a crisis such as an illness arose, however, then a worshipper might visit the shrine of a specialist deity, a god of healing, and make a sacrifice with a specific request to be returned to health. If the request was granted, then the worshipper had to fulfil whatever promise had been made to the god; this might be the dedication of an altar and many altars bear the letters VSLM: *votum soluit libens merito* (willing and deservedly fulfilled his vow), indicating a successful conclusion to an act of worship.

Most religions practised in Britain during the Roman period, for which we have evidence, were centred on the use of an altar. These were rectangular-sectioned pillars of stone with an inscription on the front of the shaft giving the name of one or more deity as well as that of the worshipper or worshippers paying for the stone. Such dedications could be made by individuals, families, military units or other groups, such as guilds. Temples often had more than one altar, three being common, but usually only one had a dish, known as the focus, carved into its top. This was to take the offerings of wine, animal's blood, oil or pinch of burning incense, which played a part in the ceremony. Altars with a focus often have roll mouldings on either side of the focus which represent, sometimes very stylistically, the bundles of incense which would have lain on a table altar (see Illustration 18). The other large altars in a temple have either flat or roughly finished tops and may have been covered with a cloth, although some show evidence for a cult statue having been fastened into position. Many have carvings on the side of the shaft depicting the equipment used in the rites and ceremonies, such as knives for sacrificing animals or jugs for pouring libations.

The dedication of a new altar was not necessary at every ceremony; some were dedicated to mark an event of special importance to the dedicator; for example, at Benwell, Tineius Longus dedicated an altar to Antenociticus in thanks for having been awarded the senatorial broad stripe, that is he had been appointed quaestor, an important step on the way to becoming a senator (*RIB* 1329). Not all dedicators were solely concerned with their own selfish needs, some dedicated for the benefit of other people, as when Afidius Eutuches and Marcus Aufidius Lemnus, both freedmen, dedicated an altar each at Bath 'for the welfare and

safety' of their master, Marcus Aufidius Maximus, a centurion in the
Sixth Legion; the discovery of these altars at a centre for healing suggests
that Marcus Aufidus Maximus was ill and his freedmen were hoping
to enlist the goddess Sulis's help in ensuring their master's recovery
(*RIB* 143, 144). It was also common for families to dedicate together
or for one of them to dedicate on behalf of their kinsfolk.

In the regular ceremonies, the deity was asked by an individual
or a group for general support through life or for a specific favour, but
occasionally the gods were more proactive and made demands on their
worshippers through a vision or dream. The Romans and native British
alike were very superstitious, and if a god appeared to someone in a
dream demanding attention, it was a foolish individual who ignored
the warning. In the case of an altar from Risingham, which bears the
inscription, 'Forewarned in a dream the soldier bade she who is married
to Fabius to set up this altar to the Nymphs who are to be worshipped'
(*RIB* 1228), the implication is that the instruction could even be given
through a third party.

Many inscriptions are by way of being 'bread-and-butter' letters,
thanking the deity concerned for benefits received, even when a vow had
not been made. These were not always for serious matters; Gaius Tetius
Veterius Micianus, prefect of the Sebosian Cavalry Regiment, for
example, dedicated an altar to the 'Unconquerable Silvanus' when he had
'killed a wild boar of remarkable fineness which many of his predecessors
had been unable to bag' (*RIB* 1041). This altar not only thanks the god
but also makes sure that everyone else is aware how skilled Micianus has
been and how he enjoys the god's favour. It was only the main altars in a
temple which were regularly used for ceremonies – the others were placed
around the walls of shrines and would have been occasionally cleared out
to make room for new dedications, as has been discovered at Maryport
in Cumbria where a group of 17 altars, dedicated to Jupiter Best and
Greatest, was found in a pit where they had been carefully deposited after
use (Breeze 1997).

Some worshippers found other ways of showing their devotion: at
Bath, Claudius Ligur 'at his own cost' had the temple of Sulis Minerva
repaired and repainted (*RIB* 141) while Sulinus, a sculptor, preferred
to dedicate a statue (*RIB* 151). At Benwell, the First Ala of Asturians
recorded their restoration of the temple to the Three Mother Goddesses
of the Parade Ground and the Genius of their Unit 'from ground level'
(*RIB* 1334).

For many religions, the eating of a communal meal was an important element in their acts of worship. Excavations at *mithraea* suggest that only young animals were consumed during these meals, possibly after they had been sacrificed to the gods. It is also evident that the animals chosen for the meals were carefully considered. At Carrawburgh *Mithraeum*, it is noticeable that the bone evidence is confined to lambs, piglets and chickens; no beef was eaten, as might be expected in a religion that had the death of the Primeval Bull as the focus of its creation myth. At the Temple to Mercury at Uley, there is a preponderance of cockerel and goat bones, the two creatures most associated with Mercury.

Native religion

Before the Romans brought their religious beliefs to Britain, the type of altar described above was not used. As the Celtic language was not a written language, the dedication of altars with inscriptions giving details of the gods and their worshippers was neither possible nor appropriate. It is because of this lack of written evidence that it is very difficult to be sure exactly how deities were worshipped in pre-Roman Britain. Traditionally, it has been presumed that the worship of the early deities was based on natural phenomena, such as groves of trees, sources of water or rock formations, and this seems to be supported by such literary evidence as there is. However, this literary evidence is either from contemporary Roman writers, who often found it difficult to understand any practises which differed from their own, or from later writers, who presumed that the religious beliefs and rites which were known in the post-Roman period in what are usually called the 'Celtic fringes', must be survivals of pre-Roman religious activity. Both groups have been used as sources for the study of the Druids.

Pliny was of the opinion that the Druidic cult started in Gaul and was imported into Britain (*Naturalis Historia* XXX.13), but Julius Caesar was sure that the route went the opposite way, commenting that 'the Druidic doctrine is believed to have been found existing in Britain and then imported into Gaul' (*De Bello Gallico* VI.13); he went on to mention that 'those who want to make a profound study of it [Druidism] generally go to Britain for the purpose'. Exactly who these Druids were, what they believed in, the names of their deities and how they conducted their ceremonies is now a confused amalgam of Roman literary devices

and more recent practises. All the Roman writers were of the opinion
that Druidic ritual involved human sacrifice, although they differed
as to the preferred method used (Henig 1984, 20), and it was for this
reason that Claudius was said to have abolished Druidism (Suetonius
Lives of the Caesars Claudius XXV.5). How successful this attempt was
is unclear; it is possible that the cult went underground and continued
to flourish, but as there is no evidence as to how widespread the cult was
before the Roman invasion, it is impossible to state precisely what affect
this edict had.

More basic religious belief may be seen in the 'Celtic heads'. These
stylised carvings are in the form of a human head, often with blank eyes
and a slit mouth, and have been identified as representing the heads
of dead warriors and linked to the Celtic veneration of the dead.
None have any inscription to clarify whether the heads are of deities
or humans, and this, coupled with the simplicity of the carving, has led
to the presumption that these are Iron Age in date. However, in recent
years, several have been found in association with Hadrian's Wall, one
actually carved on a building stone of Sewingshields milecastle, and this
may imply that 'Celtic heads' are not native British in origin but a cult
practise brought to the province by soldiers who originated in Gaul,
where the cult of the head had been long established.

Several sculptures of heads have been found with horns in the hair.
The cult of the horned head, if it be a single cult and not an
amalgamation of several different beliefs, was widespread across Europe
in pre-Roman times and continued in Britain throughout the occupation.
In Britain, there were regional variations in the way the cult figure was
perceived. The antler-bearing god may have been an import from Gaul,
where the god Cernunnos was established, as evidence for his worship
is largely limited to the south-west of Britain, particularly in the area
of the *Dobunii* where a relief from Cirencester shows a stag-horned god
in the squatting position favoured by Gallic sculptors. In the north,
a bull- or ram-horned deity, which may well be native to Britain, was
more popular and, during the Roman period, was often equated with
Mars and Mercury, as a warrior god, or with Silvanus, as a hunting
deity. This deity was often phallic, and it would appear that horned
male deities were invariably linked to fertility, whatever form they took
(Ross 1974, 172–220).

It is known that the Romans adopted deities when they encountered
them in newly conquered provinces and the lack of a written language

in Britain must have led to some problems in acknowledging the new gods accurately. When the Romans adopted the Veteres, for example, the inscriptions show that they were undecided as to the correct spelling of the name and even whether this was a god, a goddess or a whole group of deities (see *RIB* 1046–1048, 1455–1458, 1602–1606, 1697–1699) Sometimes the name is translated as 'the old gods', but the name may come from the same source as the old Nordic 'Hvitr' which means 'white' or 'shining', a term used for sun gods, or from 'Hvethr' an epithet of Loki, the German fire god. The worship of the Veteres was confined to the north of England, with a large group on Hadrian's Wall and a second group around Chester-le-Street in County Durham; this tight grouping has been taken as evidence that here is a local cult. The deity known as Belatucadrus has a similar ambiguity as to spelling as well as a similar distribution.

There has been a tendency for scholars to presume, when they encounter a deity in Britain which has not been found elsewhere in the Roman world, and which appears to have a Celtic name, that the deity must be native to Britain and has been subject to the adoption process. This is a dangerous presumption to make. As the years progressed, troops, merchants and associated travellers arrived from all over the known Roman world bringing their deities with them. Altars mentioning Coventina – a goddess long thought to be local to Carrawburgh (*Brocolitia*) on Hadrian's Wall – have recently been found in northern Spain. Did her worship travel from Carrawburgh to Spain or from Spain to Carrawburgh? An extra confusion is added when it is realised that all her worshippers who mention their ethnic origins are neither Britons nor Spaniards, but Germans. Her name is spelt in a variety of ways on the altars at Carrawburgh, which might be taken as proof of Celtic linguistic origins. Because they were all found together, we can be confident that the same deity is being invoked, but in the case of the inscriptions with slightly different spellings which have appeared in Spain or France, can we be sure that the reference is to the same goddess? It is now unclear whether Coventina was a British deity adopted by incoming Roman troops or if she came from another Roman province and was brought to Hadrian's Wall (Allason-Jones and McKay 1985).

When the Romans did adopt local gods, they seem to have expected these gods to have great powers and a very wide area of influence. Tineius Longus's dedication to Antenocitius, thanking the god for having ensured his promotion to quaestor, represents a peculiarly Roman request and begs the question as to why an ambitious Roman military man felt it was worth risking the progress of his career to a presumably native British deity (*RIB* 1329). This altar also makes it clear that while the Romans were eager to adopt new deities, they were less keen to adopt local ways of worshipping those deities. It must have been disconcerting for the local people, who may have worshipped Antenociticus all their lives, to find that under Roman rule Antenociticus had a cult statue in a stone-built temple and that his worship now involved making offerings on stone altars which bore inscriptions.

When there was some doubt about who was the right god, or the local deity's name was unknown, dedications were made to the 'genius of this place', the *genius loci*. This reflects the belief that every place had its presiding spirit, as well as an underlying worry that if a spirit was ignored, retribution would be swift.

The Roman pantheon

The invading Roman army brought with it the deities of mainstream Roman religion, and soldiers and traders of Mediterranean descent would have continued to worship their familiar gods. These deities were also regarded as the official gods of the army and as such the troops were expected to pay them due veneration, whether they came from the Mediterranean or not, whether they believed in them or not.

A case in point is Jupiter. Jupiter was the senior god in the Roman pantheon, the father of the gods, and was worshipped as the deity who protected the Roman Empire and the Roman army. Every January, army units throughout the empire would dedicate to Jupiter as a corporate act and the discovery of a series of altars at Maryport, Cumbria, shows that this could involve the dedication of a new altar (Breeze 1997). Individual soldiers showed their personal attachment to Jupiter by wearing openwork roundels on their armour which invoked Jupiter's aid or had the lightning bolts or eagles' wings associated with Jupiter painted on their shields.

Jupiter was one member of the Capitoline Triad, the others being Juno and Minerva. Juno, whose duties involved overseeing the lives of women, was not as popular in Britain as she was elsewhere in the empire: British women appear to have preferred their native deities in times of stress, but a statue of the Empress Julia Mammaea as Juno, which was found at Chesters, shows that on the frontier, the political importance of equating the empress with Juno was not unknown (*CSIR* I.6, no.117). Minerva was more popular in the province in her role as a goddess of crafts and trade, as well as wisdom and war. At Bath, she was linked, through a process called syncretism, to the local deity Sulis, who seems to have been a water deity whose worship was associated with healing springs.

The mainland of Italy was rich in deities and many of them appear to have travelled well. Thus, we find the sun god Apollo being worshipped at Chester-le-Street in County Durham (*RIB* 1043) and Whitley Castle n Northumberland (*RIB* 1198). Venus, the Roman goddess of love, appears to have been popular with the army as a deity who brought good fortune. Her role as the ancestress of the Julian family, however, may have linked her with the worship of the Deified Emperors and explain why so many pipeclay figurines of Venus have been found in military contexts.

Other deities brought from Rome included Fortuna, Mars and Diana, and inscriptions to these deities show that a very wide social group worshipped them. At York, Sosia Juncina, wife of the imperial legate, dedicated to Fortuna (*RIB* 644), but so did Antonia, the slave of Strato at Kirkby Thore (*RIB* 760). Fortuna was often present in statue form in bathhouses, as it was felt that human beings were at their most vulnerable when they were naked – it was then that they needed all the help they could get. Fortuna was particularly popular in Britain as she symbolised active good luck as well as passive protection and thus appealed enormously to the people from the Celtic provinces who were recorded as being keen gamblers.

Diana was the divine huntress and here the Celtic and Roman deities fused together: even the Romans preferred to worship Diana in a grove, rather than in a temple. Temples to Diana are rare throughout the Roman Empire, but altars, such as the one paid for by Aelia Timo at Risingham (*RIB* 1209), are known, and reliefs showing the goddess holding a bow, such as can be seen at Housesteads, have also been found (*CSIR* 1.6, no.6).

Some of these deities were worshipped by whole units as part of their military duties, just as they dedicated to Jupiter in January and to the goddess Roma, the personification of the city of Rome, on 21 April. It is difficult to understand, from a modern standpoint, whether the soldiers truly believed in the power of the gods they were marched onto the parade ground to worship or whether the authorities regarded these ceremonies as primarily bonding exercises designed to unite the troops.

Possibly, the average soldier looked on these rituals as just another of those strange things that armies do and it was not his place to question it.

The Cult of the Deified Emperors was and is peculiarly Roman and is a good example of how the Roman state used religion quite cynically as a political tool. The Roman authorities recognised at a very early stage that there was a need to weld together all the provinces of the empire, with their multitude of religious convictions, in a way which bolstered the state. This was not managed by creating a single-state religion and banning all others. This would have been counterproductive, as the provincial cults would have gone underground and worked against the state, as happened with Christianity, Judaism and Islam in twentieth-century Russia. Instead, the Cult of the Deified Emperors was instituted, and every year, all over Britain, the population had to appear at their nearest temple or meeting place to dedicate and take part in ceremonies. In this way, the Government of Rome introduced the British people to the team spirit – the team in this case being the empire.

The Cult of the Deified Emperors caused difficulties with the monotheistic cults, such as Christianity and Judaism, which recognised only one god and were sure that this god was not the emperor, but it was easily absorbed by the rest of the emperor's subjects who had been brought up to believe in lots of gods – one more or less would make little difference. Even if a man or woman was less than convinced of the divinity of the heads that they saw on their coins, they would still not have been offended and would have had little trouble going through the ceremonies.

Emperor worship was quite complex: one was not worshipping an emperor as a man, one was worshipping the essence of being an emperor. Thus, we find altars dedicated by men and women to the Emperor's Virtue, the Emperor's Fortune, and so on. By worshipping these qualities in the emperor, dedicators were worshipping the empire's virtue or fortune and by extension those qualities in themselves. It was only after death that an individual emperor could be declared a god by an act of the Senate and not all emperors were so honoured.

Eastern deities

The Roman army and travelling merchants also introduced exotic eastern deities to Britain. Jupiter Dolichenus, for example, syncretised the Roman god Jupiter with Dolichenus, the ancient Hittite thunder god.

Although his cult was never among the official cults, the worship of Jupiter Dolichenus was often linked with the health and safety of the emperor and his family and was encouraged by the authorities who considered the cult as a mechanism for fostering loyalty. Even after the main temple of Jupiter Dolichenus at Doliché was destroyed in AD 253 or 256 by the Persians, the cult went on being popular in Britain with temples still being built in the later third century.

Aesculapius was a Greek deity whose particular role was that of a healing god and as such worshipped by patients and doctors alike. At Binchester, he was worshipped by a doctor of the cavalry regiment of Vettonians, whose name can be transcribed as Marcus Aurelius Abrocomas (*RIB* 1028). The figure seen on the relief may be Abrocomas but may equally be Aesculapius. The Roman goddess of health, Salus, is also included in the dedication. Healing deities were considered essential to the continuing health of the population. By making regular dedications to such deities, worshippers attempted to ensure that they stayed healthy; if that failed, however, few doctors would expect to heal a patient if the relevant god was not supporting the curative therapy. At Lydney Park, Gloucestershire, a temple to the healing god Nodens was established in the fourth century; this included in its grounds a bathhouse and an *abaton*, a dormitory in which seekers after a cure would sleep in, in the hope that the deity would appear to them in a dream and issue instructions as to the best way to effect a cure.

Mithras was the god of light and truth in Ancient Persia and was worshipped as such by merchants at the Walbrook in London who imported marble reliefs and statuary to adorn his temple. His virtues of courage and honesty also appealed to the army, particularly to the more ambitious. The *mithraea* on Hadrian's Wall are small buildings with space for congregations of a limited size, which confirms that this was an elite cult (see Illustration 19). Comparisons between the material from these military *mithraea* and the assemblages from the other temples and shrines excavated on Hadrian's Wall reveal that, whereas on the altars to the other deities the worshippers record their ethnic origins, on the Mithraic altars the dedications reveal the military status of the worshippers. Equally, the other temples produce small artefacts which have been identified as ritual offerings made by individuals, but the *mithraea* have only produced objects which would have had a practical use in the ceremonies and rites of Mithraic worship. It is possible that some soldiers on the northern frontier in the third century AD may have regarded joining the cult as a career step, designed to bring them to the attention of officers with influence. A link between Mithraism and Freemasonry has long been recognised, and this is not the place to revisit the discussion, but, just as far-sighted young men in the nineteenth and twentieth centuries joined the Freemasons to meet people with influence and assist their careers, some Mithraic worshippers may have seen joining the cult as a shrewd career move.

This may seem to be a cynical interpretation of the evidence, but there are other examples of individuals seeking to gain secular favour by offering religious devotion. At Carvoran, for example, the following poem was inscribed on a stone plaque:

> The Virgin in her heavenly place rides upon the Lion;
> bearer of corn, inventor of law, founder of cities;
> by whose gifts it is man's good lot to know the gods;
> therefore she is the mother of the gods, Peace, Virtue,
> Ceres, the Syrian goddess, weighing life and laws in the balance.
> Syria has sent the constellation seen in the heavens to Libya
> to be worshipped: thence have we all learned.
> Thus has understood, led by thy godhead, Marcus Caecilius
> Donatianus, serving as tribune in the post of prefect by the
> Emperor's gift. (*RIB* 1791)

This dedication is ostensibly to the goddess Virgo Caelestis but identifies Julia Domna, the Syrian wife of the Libyan emperor, Septimius Severus, with Caelestis. The poem comes across as a remarkable exercise in sycophancy – Marcus Caecilius Donatianus was clearly trying to curry favour with the emperor and empress, who were in the area at the time and might see the inscription. Although there is a reference to a vision ('led by thy godhead'), one gets the impression that it was not the vision of the deity which had come to Marcus in his dreams but an idea for furthering his career.

If joining a Mithraic community was seen as an attempt to improve one's lot in a practical, rather than a purely religious way, this may explain why there are periods when there appears to be no Mithraic activity at a particular site. If the commanding officer was not a devotee, then there would be little point in joining the sect. The periodic rebuilding of the *mithraea* on Hadrian's Wall may represent the transfer to the fort of a worshipper of high enough rank to inspire the young men to join the cult. To take this further, the later attempts to re-establish a cult community at Carrawburgh may have failed because astute soldiers could see that the top people considered Christianity to be the coming religion and thus, as a consequence, there was little benefit in following Mithras.

It is unlikely that all worshippers joined a cult in the same frame of mind. In all religious communities, there will be people who believe wholeheartedly and give themselves up totally to the spiritual experience during the rites and ceremonies of their preferred religion. At the same time, several in the congregation will be wondering if their presence at the ceremony is being duly noted by the people of influence; others will be wondering if they locked the front door on their way out or if they are going to have time to dig the garden over before it starts to rain. Many of those present could fall into all these categories at some time during the same ceremony.

It would also be wrong to presume from the general attitude of the Roman government to religion that everybody respected the beliefs of all their fellow citizens. Many altars were reused by having the original inscription removed and a secondary text inscribed over the top; others might be re-used as building stones, gate posts or flooring. This would not have been seen necessarily as a profane act. An altar was regarded as a piece of religious equipment, and if it had performed its original function and the temple it was housed in had been abandoned, possibly due to the departure of the military unit which had erected it, then it would seem reasonable for it to be re-used for the worship of another god.

Initially, Christianity was seen as just another Eastern mystery cult and individual Christians may have travelled to Britain as early as the first century AD. At Carvoran, the tombstone of a woman called Aurelia Aia suggests through its plainness, its use of Christian epithets and its statement that Aelia Aia came from Salonae, a city in modern Croatia that had a very early Christian community, that this soldier's wife was a Christian (*RIB* 1828). A gold finger ring found at Corbridge in Northumberland, which bears the motto Aemilia Zeses (Aemilia may you live), may also point to an early Christian in Britain (*RIB* 2422.1; see Illustration 14). Evidence for the establishment of Christian churches with substantial and regular congregations, however, is not found until Constantine declared Christianity was to be the main religion of the Roman Empire. Throughout the fourth century, pagan cults and their temples were destroyed following a series of imperial edicts. Several temples, such as the *Mithraeum* at Housesteads, show evidence of having been deliberately destroyed at this time, although religious centres away from the military forts and large towns, such as the healing centre dedicated to Nodens at Lydney in Gloucestershire, may have carried on unmolested.

Temples and religious equipment

The Romans preferred their gods to be housed in a becoming style, and in the late first century AD, temples of all shapes and sizes sprang up in Britain from tiny shrines, such as the Shrine of the Nymphs at Carrawburgh on Hadrian's Wall, to the very large and official temples, such as that erected to the Deified Emperors at Colchester. The latter were paid for by the leading citizens of a town, who were also expected to act as priests of the imperial cult. This was a very expensive honour; according to Tacitus, 'those who had been chosen as its priests found themselves obliged to pour out their whole fortune in its service' (*Annals* XIV.31). Some cults elected their priests from among the congregation whilst others paid for professionals such as Julius Maximus, the priest at Wallsend (*RIB* 1314), and Diadora, who was the priestess of Heracles of Tyre at Corbridge (*RIB* 1129; see Illustration 20). There is increasing evidence that some of these priests decked themselves out in elaborate regalia. Crowns of chains have been found at Wanborough, Farley Heath, Stony Stratford and Cavenham Heath, while diadems have been found in some numbers at Hockwold-cum-Witton and Deeping St. James. Wooden sceptres with metal heads and metal binding around the shanks are also known; one from Farley Heath is decorated with images of animals and birds and appears to be linked to the Celtic Jupiter or a smith-god. It has been suggested that several sceptres found in East Anglia, with terminals in the form of a bearded head, were linked to the Cult of the Deified Emperors (Henig 1984, 138).

Worshippers could receive attention from their chosen deity if they contributed to the building or maintenance of the relevant temple or, like Septimius at Cirencester, provide cult statues (*RIB* 103). These acts would have the extra benefit of confirming one's status in the community, and few donations were concluded without the fact being recorded in an inscription. Some temples acted as treasuries, accepting coins or precious metal artefacts as offerings to the gods which might be used for the upkeep of the temple and its priests.

Expensive donations of silver or gold plate to the gods were only possible by the very wealthy, and even the smallest altar represented financial outlay. The less wealthy sections of society might rely on the group dedications of local worthies on behalf of the welfare of a whole town, but this lacked immediacy and would have been regarded as inadequate in times of small emergencies. The finds of sheets of lead, written on with a sharp point and then thrown into a holy pool, as at Bath and Uley, give us an insight into the religious life of the poorer inhabitants. One could use this way of communicating with the gods to ask for luck with a venture, but most requested the gods to intervene in a personal difficulty, such as the love triangle between a petitioner to Mercury at Old Harlow and Etterna and Timotneus, or to recover stolen goods and punish the perpetrator of the crime. The small amounts involved in some of these thefts indicate how little it must have cost to buy and use a curse tablet and also show how hurtful the loss of a pan or a towel could be to someone who had little to lose in the first place.

Most people's religious life was centred on the rituals carried out in the home. The Roman household god was known as the *lars familiaris*, while the *penates* were the spirits of the store cupboard. These domestic shrines came in various forms; at Verulamium (St Albans), the shrines were cupboards made of tile or stone while at Silchester a whole small room was set aside in one house and dedicated to the gods of that household. Many people relied on portable shrines made from lead or pipeclay. Members of the household would offer dedications each day and keep a light going in the shrine in honour of the household gods; in return, these gods would keep the household free from harm.

Superstition

It is in the home that we also find traces of the more primitive side of people's religious lives, that of superstition with its fear of witchcraft and magic. Some superstitions – piercing the shell of an egg or a snail once one has eaten the contents to stop evil spirits taking up residence, for example – have continued to the present day, although few people nowadays realise the antiquity of the practise or why they do it. Sorcery as an act was illegal under Roman law because magic could be used to destabilise the settled pattern of society, but the number of amulets carried by people to ward off the Evil Eye suggests that the average person, being a law-abiding citizen, preferred not to rely on witches and wizards. These amulets were expected to ward off dangers not covered by specifically named deities and many were made from stones which had unusual properties, such as the lithomarge rings and egg-shaped amulets found at Housesteads on Hadrian's Wall and Camelon in Scotland – the veins in the stone were considered powerful links to the gods. Jet and amber, being electrostatic, were also popular and had special significance for the well-being of women.

The fact that amulets and religious artefacts have been found in almost every context in Roman Britain indicates how important the population regarded its relationship with the gods. The very diverse nature of this population, however, means that there was no common religious life; every individual had their own beliefs and traditions, ceremonies and rituals which they thought proper for the veneration of the gods, and these will have varied through the centuries and depended on the origins of each worshipper.

Chapter 7
Life during the Final Years

Roman Britain was not a static place. Each generation living in the
province would have had different experiences, fears and expectations
to those of their predecessors and successors. In the first century AD, the
arrival of the Roman army would have brought chaos and devastation
for those who were caught up in the fighting but may have had little
or no immediate impact on others. The invasion of AD 43 brought major
changes in its wake, but these changes would have taken some time
to take effect throughout the whole province. During this period, there
would have been noticeable shifts in power as the old tribal leaders
either assimilated into the new Roman urban elite or lost ground to the
nouveau riche merchants and traders and the increasing numbers of
civilian administrators. These early years can be identified as a time when
the military was dominant and their inexorable advance north and west
to the outer limits of the country influenced the lives of those they came
into contact with. It was only after the Emperor Hadrian's decision
to consolidate the imperial gains, abandon Scotland for the time being
and establish a frontier between the rivers Tyne and the Solway that the
province could be said to have settled down. The annual cycle of advance
and consolidation, then withdrawal to winter quarters, with all the
disruption this entailed, was no longer part of military life. The legions
were quartered in their fortress bases, and the defence of the frontier was
largely left to the auxiliary units.

The second century can be described as the calmest period in Romano-
British history, despite Antoninus Pius's advance into Scotland and the
building of the short-lived northern frontier between the rivers Forth
and Clyde known today as the Antonine Wall. Much of our knowledge
of daily life, as described in previous chapters, comes from this period
as people were able to acquire and then lose or discard both essential and
non-essential artefacts, leaving behind them a rich artefactual record.
This was a time when shoppers and merchants could enjoy price stability
for several generations, which resulted in an expansion in material
culture involving both domestic production and imports. This was also
a time when towns had little need for defences and small farmers could

begin to expand their land holdings and farmhouses. It was only in the mid- to late third century that life became more uncertain.

Britain was divided in AD 197 into two provinces: Britannia Superior, with its capital at London; and Britannia Inferior, with its capital at York. The boundary between the two new provinces ran diagonally across the country from north of Chester to south of Leicester. The reason for this split may have been that the Emperor Septimius Severus was nervous of having an army the size of that of Britain under the command of one governor; by dividing the province he effectively halved the troops available to a potential rival. At the end of the third century, Britain was further divided into four provinces. The Verona List of AD 312–314 records these new provinces as Maxima Caesariensis, with its capital at London; Flavia Caesariensis, whose capital was probably at Lincoln; and Britannia Secunda, which was ruled from York. It has been presumed that the fourth province, Britannia Prima, had its capital at Cirencester, although Gloucester is a possible alternative; Roger White has argued that this division respected the old Iron Age tribal boundaries (2007).

In the second century, all the power was concentrated in London; after the division, there were four centres of power, each with its own governor and administrators, although London was still pre-eminent. People who had lived some distance from the administrative centre were now much closer to those who had control over their lives, and this new proximity may not always have been comfortable; the bureaucrats were now effectively large fish in much smaller ponds and may have acted accordingly. A possible fifth province, Valentia, may have been created in AD 369, with its capital at Carlisle. These divisions will have had an economic impact on the population, particularly as it has been suggested that there were customs barriers in place on the boundaries between the provinces, which would have effectively hampered trade and the free passage of people within Britain.

New dangers

Throughout the first two centuries of Roman occupation, there was little danger from enemy incursions because Britain was well protected by the size of its army and its physical separation from the Continent. In the third century, however, trouble started to brew with Rome's neighbours, many of whom became interested in acquiring land within the borders of the empire; as a consequence, troops were often withdrawn from Britain and posted elsewhere. At the same time, Britain faced new threats from all directions, and the British fleet was kept busy patrolling the waters between Britain and the Continent. During the fourth and fifth centuries, the east coast of Britain was regularly raided by Saxons, Jutes and Franks from the Continent, while the north was harried by coalitions of Picts, Scotti and Attacotti, and the north-west coast and Wales suffered raids from the tribes in Ireland.

As seen in Chapter 3, the provision of encircling walls for towns started in the late second century but these initially had been intended to protect people and property from raiding outlaws and brigands interested in seizing goods and livestock rather than a serious invasion. While being reasonably efficient, some of the walls and gates were more expressions of civic pride than serious defences. By the fourth century, however, the seriousness of the situation may be indicated by the fact that all towns and villages of any size had been provided with a defensive and defendable circuit. The addition of external interval towers in the years following the Barbarian Conspiracy of AD 367 can be taken as confirmation that an urban population was expected to defend itself with artillery or archery. An inscription from Dorchester-on-Thames, which refers to a *beneficiarius* of the governor, may be interpreted as evidence that some towns had police posts (*RIB* 235). The destruction, visible in the archaeological record of sites such as Colchester and Chelmsford, shows that towns needed their defences, while the damage seen at the villa at Preston and at many villages, such as Park Brow, indicates that the rural population was also at risk. At Caistor-by-Norwich, excavations uncovered the remains of thirty-five men, women and children who appear to have sought safety within a house which then collapsed over them.

Along the south-east coast, a series of ten heavily defended forts, known as the Saxon Shore forts, began to be established in the late third century. Some of these, such as Reculver Fort, Burgh Castle, Portchester Castle and Lympne Castle, were new builds, whereas the existing forts at Dover and Richborough were either rebuilt or refortified. These forts appear to have been a response to increased raiding by the Saxons; however, there is no evidence that any of the forts were continuously occupied, so the threat may have been intermittent. Along the north-east coast, a series of coastal fortlets, such as Goldsborough, were erected around the same time, probably to provide an early warning system against raiders from the sea. There were also new or refurbished coastal installations at Lancaster and Caer Gyby in Wales.

Economy

Political events, both those confined to Britain and those which took place elsewhere in the empire, began to have an impact on the Romano-British economy. The problems for the empire as a whole may have started with the murder of Gordian III in AD 244, as this was followed by a period of forty years when fifty-five emperors were proclaimed. In AD 293, the empire was divided into two by Diocletian. This separation into an Eastern Empire and a Western Empire, each with its own emperor and power base, reduced the resources that each had available and encouraged rivalries between the two sets of ruling elites. A number of weak emperors in the late fourth century AD, such as Julian (AD 360–363) and Honorius (AD 395–423), compounded the problems. On the other hand, each emperor now had a smaller area under his rule, and some, such as Valentinian and Theodosius, provided periods of stable and efficient rule.

The population of a country usually becomes concerned about political crises only when inflation starts to bite and affects them personally. During the third century AD, a number of such crises had an impact on the Roman currency, and as it became increasingly difficult to acquire the supplies of bullion needed to mint new coins, the Roman government began to debase the silver content; this debasement led to the collapse of the Augustan monetary system between AD 260 and 270, a system which had remained reasonably stable for around 400 years. This process can be seen in Britain through the large numbers of *denarii*, many counterfeit, that are found in early-third-century contexts before the *denarius* was gradually replaced as the basic denomination by the *antoninianus* or 'radiate' in the middle and later third century. This new coin had a minimal silver content, which led to older silver coinage being hoarded. *Sestertii* were no longer minted as inflation became increasingly rampant, and large quantities of 'radiate copies' were produced in the province to provide much-needed small change.

During the late third century, the economy continued to be unstable, and this instability is discernible in the archaeological record. In excavations, there is a sudden surge in the number of coins found on sites of all types around AD 260–270, reflecting the fact that as the purchasing power of the coins fell, large numbers were needed to carry out any sizable purchase. The value of individual coins was now so low that it was hardly worth the bother of picking up any that were dropped. Many short-lived coin issues followed, as successive emperors tried to remedy the situation, and these can be observed by plotting coin finds; before AD 260–270, the plots show only slight changes, but after this period the graphs show dramatic peaks and troughs. When Diocletian came to the throne in AD 284, he introduced a number of economic reforms that would have affected people's lives, such as a price edict which decreed how much commodities should cost and how much craftsmen should be paid for their services anywhere in the empire. He also began the process of separating the civil government of provinces from their military command, the latter now being under the control of *duces*. It is not known when this separation was instituted in Britain, as an inscription from Birdoswald shows that the governor was still in control at the time of Constantius (*RIB* 1912).

Between AD 378 and 388, the number of new coins being minted was reduced, and barter began to play as important a part in the economic life of the province as coinage. This move from a monetary economy to a barter system affected the military as their wages could not keep pace with inflation. By the late third century, a soldier's pay in Britain was no longer enough to cover his subsistence. For a while, the shortfall was made up by donatives of gold or silver plus occasional payments on the accession of a new emperor (and thereafter at five-yearly intervals) or to mark special events. By the fourth century, three-quarters of the military was paid in kind, which would have had a knock-on effect for those who relied on the army for financial support or who made their living by supplying the military with their needs.

When faced with unpredictable inflation, ordinary people tend to use their money cautiously. In Britain, the number and range of artefacts found in excavations diminish noticeably during the fourth century. Fewer imported items are to be found in excavated assemblages, more items show evidence of repair and fewer luxury items appear. Analysis of pottery found on sites of the period also emphasises these economic difficulties. Most imported pottery ceases to appear in the archaeological record between AD 250 and 275, although Campanian wine amphorae and a form of pottery known as *ceramique à l'époge* only start to be popular around AD 275 and continue to be so until around AD 325. The internal pottery trade underwent several changes as well. In the south-east, large centres of production gave way to small potteries making handmade vessels with a limited distribution. By AD 300, the only potteries supplying the frontier on Hadrian's Wall are the black-burnished industries of Dorset, the Nene Valley and East Yorkshire; so it must be concluded there was not a large enough military population in the north to support more than a basic pottery output. This reduction in their market would have had a serious impact on the economy of the production centres, and many people will have found themselves unemployed. At the very end of the fourth century, Crambeck reduced ware was finally overtaken in the north as the dominant pottery type by calcite-gritted ware. This change in the preferred pottery type does not just mean that there was a new source but that the types of vessels supplied were noticeably different. The Crambeck ware had been available in a range of forms, but the calcite-gritted ware was only used for cooking pots. As Paul Bidwell (personal communication) has pointed out, this limitation in the forms available to customers may be interpreted as a shift to simpler cooking techniques; there was no longer a need for or an interest in the specialisation that characterised Roman cuisine (see Chapter 5). Without pottery, most households would have reverted to using bronze, which could be easily recycled when beyond repair, or wood or leather vessels, which leave few archaeological traces.

There is evidence that other large industries collapsed, such as mining and quarrying. These extractive industries were under imperial control, and anyone wishing to invest in mining required a licence, which may have become increasingly difficult to obtain. Moreover, their products needed military protection if they were to be delivered safely to customers. This protection would have become unavailable if troops were withdrawn from the province or were already fully occupied defending the coastline or the northern frontier. Initially, this would have impacted only building programmes and the people who were employed in quarries and mines, but eventually the dwindling supplies of metal and stone would have resulted in problems for ordinary householders. It is noticeable that few specialised tools were used in the fourth century and that knives increasingly became the tool of choice. The reason for this development may be that, as the mines ceased production and the raw material became scarce, a workman would have found a multi-purpose tool, such as a knife, more cost-effective than a range of individual tools with defined purposes, which required greater amounts of metal and, therefore, were expensive.

In the north, the nature of the forts on Hadrian's Wall seems to have changed in the fourth century. At Newcastle upon Tyne, for example, there is evidence that a market was established on the *via principia* between AD 330 and 370, suggesting that the fort may not have been an exclusively military establishment during this period, although it had been returned to military use by the end of the fourth century. The size of the garrisons in those forts that were occupied appears to have been halved, probably as a result of the activities of various emperors in Gaul and Germany which had made calls on the units stationed in Britain. Some of the field army, the *comitatenses*, had been taken from Britain in the AD 380s by Magnus Maximus, but the *limitanei*, the frontier troops, probably continued in the role of a frontier police force. Maintenance programmes on Hadrian's Wall were undertaken by drafts of civilian workmen from the *Durotriges*, *Dumnonii* and *Catuvellauni* tribes from the south, suggesting that there were not enough military personnel in position to carry out the work (*RIB* 1672, 1673, 1843, 1962). How these people were recruited is not known. Most of the *vici* on Hadrian's Wall were reduced to a few houses or none at all some time in the third century, while the more northerly villas, such as Old Durham, Dalton-on-Tees, Middleham and Snape, were also abandoned by their owners. The small town of Sedgefield in County Durham has produced no evidence of fourth-century occupation and may well have become a ghost town by the later third century.

There were some people, however, who were able to prosper. In the north, the open settlements at Long Newton, Newton Bewley and Seaton Carew – which might be more accurately described as farms rather than villas – do manage to survive into the fourth century. At the same time, in the south-east, hoards of gold and silver plate and jewellery were being buried, indicating that some people were able to afford elaborate possessions. The Hoxne hoard, for example, includes not only elaborate openwork bracelets and silver spoons but also a gilded pepper pot in the shape of a female bust, an item only useful if its owner was able to afford imported spices. Why these hoards were buried is open to speculation. One reason may have been that the wealthy were hoarding disposable wealth as the economy collapsed, but it is also possible that, faced with incursions from invading troops, householders were trying to ensure that their valuables were safe from discovery. The religious iconography of many of the items in the hoards may indicate other reasons.

In the late third century, while some people were experiencing
financial problems, a few villa owners appear to have become extremely
wealthy and their town and country houses and estates became very large
and sumptuously decorated. This is a phenomenon which can be noted
throughout history; when a country is experiencing economic decline,
there is always a small elite which flourishes and flaunts its wealth.
In Roman Britain, these wealthy estate owners, whatever their ethnic
origins, seem to have developed a nostalgia for the glory days of the early
empire, particularly the Augustan period. This nostalgia is evident
in references to the works of Virgil and Ovid in the interior decoration
of the larger villas. The interest in classical literature may have been the
result of the political activities which now pushed Britain into the empire-
wide spotlight. The usurper Carausius, who declared himself emperor
of a breakaway Britain in AD 286, issued a silver coin that bore the legend
'come, long-awaited one', a quote from Virgil's *Aeneid* that reveals much
about Carausius's psychology. It also declared his manifesto for the
empire: there was to be a new age of prosperity for the empire and
anyone who supported him would prosper in his empire. Carausius's
plans came to a sudden end when he was murdered by his Finance
Minister, Allectus, in AD 293, although Britain was not restored to the
Roman Empire until Allectus in his turn was defeated by Constantine I
in AD 296.

As homes, such as at Great Casterton and North Wraxall, were
destroyed by invaders and the economy floundered, the early years
of the fifth century may have witnessed continual population movements
throughout the country. Many of the rural population will have moved
into towns to seek security behind the substantial stone walls; others
may have taken advantage of the proximity of an Iron Age hillfort
and re-occupied it. The collapse of many industries would have led
to craftsmen travelling to seek new employment or giving up their skills
to join a mercenary unit. There would also have been continual troop
movements as soldiers were moved from one danger zone to another
or shipped abroad. The *Notitia Dignitatum* lists a number of British units
serving on the Continent, Egypt or the East at this time. Claudian records
Stilicho removing a British legion in AD 401–402 to assist in the defence
of Italy against Alaric, although this may have been an exaggeration.
More troops were removed by the usurper Constantine III in AD 406–407,
but there is no evidence for a complete military withdrawal under any
emperor.

The destruction of standing crops during skirmishes by raiding parties and the abandonment of land in the face of danger would have led to a shortage of food supplies. The perils of shipping in the English Channel and the unwillingness of the wealthy to invest in trade, due to the uncertainty of the financial situation, would have limited the import of food to supplement any short-term difficulties. The story of a famine in the territory of the *Dumnonii* in the sixth century, which was only relieved by the arrival of an Alexandrian grain ship, is unlikely to have been an unusual situation (Wacher 1974, 335). Wacher has put forward the theory that Britain may also have faced a number of epidemics around the beginning of the fifth century AD (1974, 415). Epidemics and pandemics would have had most effect on the urban populations and probably contributed to the demise of several towns. Throughout Britain, it would have become increasingly difficult to maintain normal family life as both military and civilian families were split up, danger threatened on all sides and a steady income became increasingly difficult to sustain. Excavations at Birdoswald suggest that some people gathered together under the protection of a local leader, either someone who had a traditional right to their loyalty or a new warlord.

The impact of Christianity

Did Christianity provide some reassurance of stability in an increasingly unstable world or was it seen as the cause of that instability? The Roman takeover of Britain had been made less painful by its open-minded attitude to different religions, but when Christianity was declared by law to be the sole religion of the whole empire and pagan temples were destroyed by imperial edict, many people must have found their lives turned upside down. As this event coincided with attacks along the coastline and the collapse of the economy, it is easy to see how some Britons might have seen cause and effect between the official abandonment of the old gods and these new dangers and abandoned Christianity as soon as it was safe to do so.

Christianity had been introduced into the country as early as the second century AD, but it took a while to be regarded by most of the population as anything other than an ordinary eastern mystery cult (Thomas 1981). Anti-Christian sentiment, possibly caused by the religion's worshippers'

refusal to accept any other religion but their own and by their unwillingness to participate in imperial cult events, led to the religion being
driven underground throughout the third century. It was not until the
early fourth century that Christians could feel confident enough to build
churches and martyria to those who had suffered persecution under the
reigns of Decius and Valerius. In AD 313, the Edict of Milan declared
Christianity to be the official religion of the Roman Empire. By AD 314,
the British church was already established enough to send three bishops,
a priest and a deacon to the Council of Arles, one representing each of
the provinces of Britain. By AD 359, Britain was able to send twenty-five
delegates to the Council of Ariminum, although poverty meant that three
of them had to accept free transport from Constantius II.

Several buildings at the forts of Vindolanda, South Shields,
Housesteads and Birdoswald have been identified as being Christian
churches, and the discovery of a number of artefacts, in particular a small
portable altar at Vindolanda, suggest that the army followed the official
diktat as to the new status of Christianity. This acceptance of Christianity
may have been more a matter of obeying orders or following the lead
of the commanding officers rather than a heartfelt religious conversion
on the part of individual soldiers. Excavations of temples on the frontier
reveal clear evidence that the army, whatever their motives, carried
out the Edicts of Theodosius in regard to pagan worship and cult
centres efficiently and to the letter: Coventina's Well, the *mithraea*
at Housesteads and Carrawburgh and the Shrine to the Nymphs and
Genii Loci, also at Carrawburgh, show unequivocal evidence of
deliberate closure and desecration. In the civilian south, however,
despite its appealing promise of a better life after death for all, whether
man or woman, slave or free, rich or poor, Christianity seems to have
been particularly favoured by the urban aristocracy who decorated both
their town houses and their villas with Christian images in mosaic and
wall painting. Certainly the religion relied heavily on its richer members
to provide the silver and pewter plate used in ceremonies.

While Christianity was now the official religion of the empire and
all pagan cults were banned by law, in Britain there seems to have been
a curious situation that new pagan temples were still being erected.
An example is the healing complex dedicated to the god Nodens, which
was built at Lydney in Gloucestershire. This may be the result of the
Emperor Julian repealing the anti-pagan laws around this time or may
suggest that Christianity did not have as tight a grip on Britain as

elsewhere in the empire. The hoard of treasure found at Thetford in Norfolk, which was buried at the very end of the fourth century AD, contains several cult objects dedicated to an ancient Latin woodland god Faunus: possibly another example of the fashion for nostalgia and recalling earlier, better times.

The new legitimacy of Christianity may have had a more fundamental impact on the inhabitants of Britain than just fulfilling a spiritual need or denying access to the old gods. The belief that the body had to be preserved so that it could be resurrected on the Day of Judgement led to inhumation replacing cremation as the preferred burial practice, often with the bodies preserved in gypsum. Theoretically, the adoption of Christianity should have been accompanied by a sudden lack of grave goods, as the provision of objects to accompany the deceased to the afterlife was frowned upon by the Christian church. However, evidence is increasingly emerging that, in the fourth century, many Christians were conservative when it came to their own burials. At York, for example, one grave included perfume bottles and jewellery as well as an openwork bone plaque with the motto 'Hail Sister, May You Live in God'. Silver plaques, such as that from Chesterton in Cambridgeshire, which has a ChiRho symbol along with an inscription which reads 'Iancilla fulfilled the vow that she promised' (*RIB* 2431.1), suggest that British Christians saw little difference in the mechanics of worshipping their god from the earlier worship of pagan deities.

The strictures of the early Christian writers decreed how people, particularly women, should dress and comport themselves. This, as will be discussed below, would have had a noticeable impact on the appearance of the population. The use of cosmetics and elaborate hairstyles, even attention to basic hygiene, was now considered unacceptable. These writers also disapproved of contraception, abortion and infanticide, which may have led to an increase in birth rates, with its associated medical and economic effects on families.

Personal appearance

In the first and second century AD, there were several pictorial tomb-stones and statues which give an impression of what the population might have looked like. In the third century, however, these cease to be produced, and we have to rely on archaeological evidence to suggest what people were wearing and how they might have dressed their hair. This evidence indicates that there were differences in appearance between the early and later populations of Roman Britain. For example, the bodies of fourth-century women found in the province show a remarkable lack of objects associated with them that could have been used to confine or pin the hair. Hilary Cool (2000) has pointed out 'the plummeting position of hairpins' in the lists of grave finds through the fourth century. She identified hairpins in the mid-fourth century as forming 41 percent of the total assemblages, but by the late fourth century this had dropped to only 10 percent. Tertullian was of the opinion that a coiled bun was the only suitable hairstyle for a Christian woman, but even the simplest of buns requires a hairpin or two (*On Female Dress* VII). This lack of pins could be taken as an indication that women either used only wooden pins or that they no longer wore their hair up in complicated styles.

From about AD 326 onwards, it became the fashion for women to cover their hair, whether in the house or outside, with a veil. This may not have been an entirely voluntary fashion as St. Paul, in First Corinthians, stated that a woman should wear her hair covered as a symbol of her husband's authority over her. In the late fourth century, the light veil was often replaced by an enveloping cap. If this was normal day-to-day wear, there was little point in having a fancy hairstyle, with or without decorations, and it is possible that most women's hair was simply coiled under the cap or pinned with very simple pins.

From sculpture elsewhere in the empire, we can suggest that by the late third century the most popular hairstyle for men was what today would be called a crew cut, with a very short beard, almost designer stubble, which was trimmed on the neck but not shaved away entirely. From the time of Constantine, however, being completely clean shaven seems to have been preferred, with the hairstyles reverting to those of the early empire with short curls brushed forward. In the fourth century, the curls were replaced by straight hair worn combed down from the crown in the 'pudding basin' style.

These styles, of course, are what would have been worn by those men who followed Mediterranean fashions. What is unclear is what was being worn by the *comitatenses*, the *limitanei* or the *numeri*, who may have preferred the hairstyles of their homelands. After all, it has been shown from Trajan's Column that in the early imperial period Hamian archers preferred wearing their hair long, as well as their skirts, and it is possible that soldiers in the later units, drafted in from the peripheries of the empire, such as the *numerus Hnaudifridi*, may have worn Swabian knots or other individualised styles.

Beaded necklaces were worn throughout the Roman period, but there is a noticeable change in the colour and types of beads being used in the fourth century, with very small blue and green beads being worn as well as false pearls, made from clear glass enclosing gold or silver foil. There was also a sharp rise in the use of jet and other black materials for beads. This is particularly noticeable at York, where the fashion may be linked to the cult of Bacchus having a last stand in the face of the rise of Christianity. Black material was also popular for finger rings at this time. Bronze and iron finger rings have been found in fourth century contexts, but these rarely hold intaglios. In fact, of sixty-one intaglios from Vindolanda only one can be assigned to a fourth-century context. This may be because there were fewer people on the northern frontier with a Roman understanding of what an intaglio was for or fewer people who were qualified to wear one.

In the fourth century, women no longer appear to have been dependent on brooches for maintaining their modesty, but equally both sexes appear to have been less inclined to use brooches for sheer adornment. At this period, the wide range of brooches available in the second and early third centuries suddenly contracts to two basic types: the penannular brooches, which may have been used by women to secure their clothing, and the substantial crossbow brooches, which seem to have been used only by men and may have denoted the status of their wearers. It is possible that some of the earlier brooches may have been intended more as badges, signifying membership of a cult or a guild; as Christianity became dominant, these may have become inappropriate.

In the mid-fourth century, the bracelet assemblages tend to be about 50:50 jet or shale versus bronze with a few made of bone for the first time. The sheer quantity found at South Shields and York makes it clear that the women of the frontier had a preference for black bracelets by the mid-fourth century, having abandoned the lighter colours of the glass bracelets by the end of the second century. By the later fourth century, however, the number of black bracelets in excavations drops noticeably while the number of copper alloy examples grows. These were mostly made of twisted strands of wire or basic strips with incised or chip-carved decoration and hook-and-eye fastenings. Evidence from grave assemblages in York suggests that a woman might own quite a few of these and that they were probably worn in groups, which would, of course, affect the numbers found.

From this evidence, two major changes might be postulated in female appearance in this late period. First, there is an increased fashion for wearing black jewellery; whether these decorations were made of jet, shale, cannel coal or detrital coal seems to have been immaterial. Second, there was an increase in the amount of cheap jewellery worn. We may be forgiven for imagining, from the discovery of the famous hoards at Hoxne and Thetford, that everyone in the south of the country was either wearing gold or hoarding it; in the north there is no hint that there was much interest in gold or even silver jewellery.

There was also a change in how people sounded as they moved. The number of bronze bracelets worn would mean that most women would have been heard coming from some distance – they would have looked different but they would also have sounded different as their bracelets rattled. It is also probable that the administrators and military men who wore pretentious metal belt sets and strap ends in the fourth century would have been fully aware that their impressive appearance was enhanced by the accompanying, somewhat menacing, clash of metal as they walked.

In the south-east of Britain, wall paintings and mosaics occasionally give us information about the colour of the clothing worn. Lullingstone villa, in particular, depicts men wearing tunics with decorative bands of contrasting colours (see Illustration 21). Unfortunately, few textile fragments have survived from later contexts to support the presumption that coloured clothing, manufactured using locally derived dyestuffs, continued to be popular. It is, however, possible that the rise in Christianity had an impact on dress colours. The early Christian fathers did not approve of the wearing of coloured clothing; the colours of wool and linen in their natural state were considered to be quite good enough. Tertullian even went so far as to aver that if God had wanted people to wear purple and sky blue clothes, He would have created purple and sky blue sheep (*On Female Dress* VIII).

The actual garments worn probably did not change in any particularly noticeable way, although there was obviously no longer a need for chained brooches to hold women's tunics together, as there had been in the second and third centuries, which suggests a slightly different design. Both men and women will have continued to wear variations on a tunic. In Rome, the clothing of emperors and empresses altered to more elaborate dress; for example, a type of decorated toga, called a *trabea*, was worn by the male ruling classes from the mid-fourth century onwards, but this was to set them apart and would have had little impact on the day-to-day dress of the provincial civilian populations. There is evidence that men and women from the third century onwards wore a long sleeved tunic called a *dalmaticus*, which was worn unbelted, and women took advantage of this to wear their skirts shorter than before. Other women wore a girdle high up under the bust. Over this might be worn a new kind of mantle, sometimes decorated with heavily embroidered strips.

Postscript

The end of Britain as a Roman province is usually dated to AD 410, a year in which the Emperor Honorius is reported as having written to the city fathers of the empire to inform them that their protection was now in their own hands (Zosimus *Historia Nova* VI.5-2). This is often taken to include a direct instruction to the province of Britain, although the word 'Brettia' may not have referred to Britain at all but to the southern Italian town of Brittunum. The failure of the troops' pay to arrive during that year may have had more impact on the inhabitants of Britain, although it is difficult to ascertain how many soldiers would have been affected if the bulk of their pay was already in kind.

Three of the four provinces of Britain did not survive the fifth century, but Roger White (2007) has argued that Britannia Prima, particularly that section now covered by the principality of Wales, did survive. Discoveries of military fittings with a Germanic appearance are confined to the eastern side of the country, not the Irish settled areas in the west, suggesting that Britannia Prima had its own adequate army, 'possibly stiffened by a core of Irish warriors, such as Cunorix' from Wroxeter (White 2007). The survival of the towns at Wroxeter and Chester may indicate that there were attempts to keep Roman urban life going.

White points out that the level of early Anglo-Saxon occupation in Britain varies from province to province. The Franks, Saxons and Jutes settled in Maxima Caesariensis, Angles in Flavia Caesariensis, the Angles and Scandinavians in Britannia Secunda and the Irish in Britannia Prima. The far south-west of Britain had never really accepted *Romanitas* in its entirety, and the people of this region may have had strong trade links to the Continent, due to their ability to provide tin, which gave them independent power. This may explain why Mediterranean pottery as late as the sixth century AD has been found at Tintagel, Dinas Powys and South Cadbury.

The incursions by the Anglo-Saxon raiders in the fourth and fifth centuries have often been suggested as major contributors to the fall of Roman Britain. Michael Jones (1996), however, has pointed out that Anglo-Saxon settlement in Britain only began around AD 430, twenty years after the traditionally recognised end of Roman Britain. He has further emphasised that the new migrants could have numbered no more than 100,000 against a possible existing population of 3 million – numbers which suggest that the 'invaders' could have had only a minimal impact on the whole country, although their presence would have affected the lives of those who were living in the immediate areas of their landings.

A. S. Esmonde-Cleary (1989) was also of the opinion that invasion was not the whole answer to the question as to why Britain ceased to be a province of the Roman Empire. He saw the end as an element in the broader context of imperial politics and the result of economic collapse. He argued that Rome lost control of a number of lands in the western provinces in the early fifth century and that these losses disrupted the collection of taxes. This fiscal situation meant that Rome could no longer afford to maintain an army in Britain.

Martin Millett (1990) argued that the end of Britain as a Roman province was the result of a revolt by the elite who resented paying taxes, particularly as the army these taxes were meant to pay for could no longer protect the British people. Thompson (1984), however, held the alternative view that the revolt came from the *bacaudae* or peasants. Dark (1994, 2000) believed that these scenarios rely too heavily on the political causes for the demise of Roman Britain and ignore the cultural and social traditions which would have contributed to the situation.

Whichever model one accepts for the final end of Roman Britain, it is clear that it was not a sudden end brought on by invasions from outside peoples, as was once believed, but a slow decline resulting from political and economic factors, with possible contributions from disease and famine. Faced with increasing instability, Britain could no longer supply the natural resources that had made the country such a prize for Julius Caesar and Claudius. Rome had its own problems with barbarian invaders; Britain's difficulties gradually became of less and less political and economic importance to the Roman emperors and government, and

it is not surprising that eventually the province was cut adrift to cope
on its own.

Whether the rest of the empire regretted the loss of Britain is another
question. There is a hint in some of the later Latin literature that the
Britons were not well thought of by the rest of the Roman Empire. Even
in neighbouring Gaul, the Britons were increasingly seen as being
treacherous and unreliable. This may, of course, be due to the many
rebellions which started in Britain, led by such usurpers as Carausius and
Magnus Maximus. Ausonius of Bordeaux, for example, a man
of influence in fourth-century Gaul, wrote a series of epigrams, one
of which reads:

What? Silvius Good?
No Briton could
Be – better he had
Been Silvius Bad.

This refers to a British poet Silvius Bonus and is not the only indication
that Britons had a poor standing among their neighbours. The
theological writer Pelagius also found that his British origins gave his
enemies good ammunition to attack his writings. By the end of the fifth
century, Gildas was of the opinion that the Britons were made up of
historically antagonistic separate groups and no good would come of
them until they mended their ways.

Legacy

It is noticeable that, whatever the reason for the collapse of the Roman
provinces of Britannia, some traces of its existence disappeared quite
quickly. Many of the major civil engineering projects required peace and
a well-run administration to build and sustain. Without a well-run tax
system and an efficient bureaucracy, the maintenance of the roads,
bridges, public bathhouses, water and sewerage systems and town
defences would have ground to a halt. Initially, this would have had little
effect but with time the lack of repairs would have led to irreversible
deterioration.

The speed at which the norms of a Roman province crumbled – within
a generation most of the 'benefits' of Roman rule had either disappeared
or were in a state of considerable disrepair – raises the question of how
Roman the British population had become. How well had they developed

into proper Roman citizens since the Claudian invasion? The answer may be that many of the trappings of life which we today identify as 'being Roman' may have just been skin deep or appreciated only by those who were wealthy enough to afford them or in whose political interests it was to maintain them.

The lifestyle of the wealthy villa owners also required a stable political situation. Fine dining demanded imported food and wine, elaborate tableware and staff to serve guests. Any political disruption invariably resulted in an interruption to imports and possibly to a host's financial ability to throw expensive parties. The threat of invasion would have dissuaded guests from travelling away from home and accepting invitations. As for bathing, a Roman bathhouse required staff to stoke the fires and the leisure of the bathers to enjoy the experience, neither of which was possible in a country whose inhabitants were in daily expectation of being attacked by barbarians.

There is evidence that some aspects of Roman culture carried on. St. Augustine's claim that Roman culture had to be reintroduced to Britain in the late sixth century may have been a political statement referring to the Roman as opposed to the Celtic church which was in the ascendancy. When St. Germanus of Auxerre visited the shrine of St. Alban in AD 429, he found the magistrates and citizens to be splendidly dressed and enjoying a comfortable lifestyle. The writings of Gildas and St. Patrick reveal that they lived in literate societies which were still used to speaking both Latin and Celtic.

The date of the collapse of town life may not be very clear as the public buildings would be of stone and would take some time to completely disintegrate. It is also difficult to identify when such buildings were reused for living quarters, although some show clear signs of being reused for industrial purposes. In London, the demolition of the great public buildings and the incorporation of their stonework into the Riverside Wall in the early fourth century, which was seen as evidence of urban decay, has now been identified as being the result of changes in the river levels; the tidal point no longer came as far as the waterfront used in the second century AD, so the merchant area moved east and established a new port on the Pool of London where the river was deeper. The success of this venture may be deduced from the size of the *mansio* baths recently excavated at Shadwell and by the discovery of a late basilica at Colchester House on Tower Hill. Other ventures were less successful.

Town life was a Roman phenomenon, as was discussed in Chapter 3, so the failure of urban activity in Britain can be taken as an indicator of the end of Britain as a Roman entity. However, it is clear that each town experienced a different fate in the late fourth and early fifth centuries. While there is evidence that the towns in the east, such as Lincoln, Colchester and Canterbury, may have fallen to the Anglo-Saxons early on, others may have carried on for some time, building timber structures to replace the crumbling stonework. However, life in these towns was now a far cry from that in the efficiently run urban centres of the second century. As Wacher has stated, 'Town life had been reduced to life in towns' (1974, 422), and daily life for Britons was never to be the same again.

Timeline

c.100   Portland and Hengistbury Head develop
as trading ports.

58–51   Roman conquest of Gaul.

58–57   Gallic nobles seek sanctuary with tribal chieftains
in Kent and Sussex.

55–54   Julius Caesar's expeditions to Britain.

30   Octavian becomes sole ruler and Emperor.

c.15   Coinage of Tasciovanus appears.

AD

7   Tincommius flees to Rome.

40   Gaius Caligula's planned invasion of Britain aborted.

43   Invasion of Britain by Claudius.

47   Roman conquest of south and east of England
completed.

49–50   Foundation of *Colonia Victricensis* at Colchester
(*Camulodunum*).

c.50   Foundation of London (*Londinium*).

59–60   Roman attack on the Druidic centre on Anglesey.

60–61   Boudiccan revolt.

66   *Legio XIV Gemina* withdrawn from Britain.

71   *Legio II Adiutrix* posted to Britain.

71–74   Establishment of legionary fortress at York (*Eburacum*).

75–80   Mosaics first appear in domestic buildings in Britain.

81   Agricola reaches the Forth–Clyde isthmus.

83–84   Battle of Mons Graupius.

85	*Legio II Adiutrix* transferred to the Danube.
90–96	Foundation of *Lindum Colonia* at Lincoln.
96–98	Foundation of *Colonia Nervia Glevensium* at Gloucester.
c.100	Scotland largely abandoned. Northern frontier now on the Stanegate between the rivers Tyne and Solway.
107/108	Last inscriptional reference to *Legio IX Hispana* in Britain.
122	Visit of Emperor Hadrian to Britain. Work starts on building Hadrian's Wall. *Legio VI Victrix* posted to Britain.
140–143	Quintus Lollius Urbicus advances into Scotland. The Antonine Wall is built.
c.155	Antonine Wall abandoned and Hadrian's Wall re-commissioned. Verulamium largely destroyed by fire.
193–197	Britain under the rule of Clodius Albinus, creating a brief splinter empire.
197	Edict of Emperor Septimius Severus allows serving soldiers the right to marry.
205–208	Britain is divided into two provinces: Britannia Superior and Britannia Inferior.
208	Septimius Severus arrives in Britain with his family and prepares to advance into Scotland.
211	Septimius Severus dies in York. The attempt to conquer Scotland is abandoned.
212	Caracalla becomes emperor by killing his brother. Caracalla decrees all freeborn provincials are now Roman citizens.
259–274	Britain under the rule of the Gallic emperors.
260–270	Final collapse of Augustan monetary system.

270s	Establishment of Saxon Shore forts.
280–324/326	London has its own coin mint.
287	Carausius, commander of the Channel Fleet, proclaims himself emperor.
294	Carausius is murdered by his Finance Minister Allectus.
295	Britain is restored to the empire after the defeat of Allectus by Constantius Chlorus.
296	Britain divided into four provinces during Diocletian's reorganisations, which also separates military and civil administration.
305/306	Constantius Chlorus campaigns in Scotland. After his death in York his son Constantine is proclaimed emperor at York by his father's soldiers.
312–314	Verona List records the names of Britannia's four new provinces.
313	Edict of Milan decrees Christianity to be the official religion of the Roman Empire.
314	Three British bishops attend Council of Arles.
345–350	Count Gratian sent to Britain to command the army.
350–353	Britain under the rule of the Gallic usurper Magnentius.
359	British bishops at Council of Ariminum (Rimini).
360	Julian sends fourteen field units to Britain after raids on the frontier by Scots and Picts.
360–363	Emperor Julian ships grain from Britain.
364	Raids of Picts, Scotti, Attacotti and Saxons.
367	The Barbarian Conspiracy.
369	Possible creation of fifth province, Valentia, with its capital at Carlisle.
383	Usurpation of Magnus Maximus begins in Britain and then moves to Gaul.

391	Edict of Emperor Theodosius bans all pagan worship.
394–408	Stilicho is commander-in-chief of the western armies.
395	Death of Theodosius leads to division between eastern and western empires.
402	Official import of newly minted bronze coins to Britain ceases.
406	Rhine–Thames trade disrupted in Germany by tribal invasions.
407	Further units of troops removed from Britain by the usurper Constantine III.
408	Effective Roman rule in Britain ceases when Britain revolts from Constantine III.
410	Emperor Honorius writes to council elders of 'Brettia' to state that they would henceforth be responsible for their own protection.
411	Constantine III assassinated.
430	Anglo-Saxon settlement begins in eastern Britain.

List of Figures

List of Illustrations

18. Altar to Antenociticus from Benwell showing focus, mouldings and knife. Museum of Antiquities of the University and Society of Antiquaries of Newcastle upon Tyne.

19. The reconstruction of Carrawburgh Mithraeum. Museum of Antiquities of the University and Society of Antiquaries of Newcastle upon Tyne.

20. Figurine of a priestess from South Shields. Museum of Antiquities of the University and Society of Antiquaries of Newcastle upon Tyne.

21. Lullingstone *orantes* wallpainting. British Museum.

22. Page from *Notitia Dignitatum*. Bodleian Library.

Bibliography

Abu-Lughod, J. 1969. 'Migrant Adjustment to City Life: The Egyptian Case'. In *The City in Newly Developing Countries*. Edited by G. Breese, Princeton, pages 376–388.

Allason-Jones, L. 2003. 'The Jet Industry and Allied Trades in Roman Britain'. In *Aspects of Industry in Roman Yorkshire and the North*. Edited by P. Wilson and J. Price, Oxford, pages 12–32.

Allason-Jones, L. 2005a. *Women of Roman Britain*, 2nd ed. York.

Allason-Jones, L. 2005b. 'Germs and the Roman Army in Britain'. In *Limes XIX: Proceedings of the XIXth International Congress of Roman Frontier Studies*. Edited by Z. Visy, Budapest, Hungary, September 2003, pages 309–313.

Allason-Jones, L. forthcoming. *Artefacts in Roman Britain: Their Purpose and Use*. Cambridge.

Allason-Jones, L., and B. McKay. 1985. *Coventina's Well*. Chollerford.

Applebaum, S. 1972. 'Roman Britain'. In *The Agrarian History of England and Wales*, vol. 1. ii. Edited by H. P. R. Finberg, Cambridge.

Austen, R. G. 1934. 'Roman Board-Games'. *Greece and Rome* 4: 24–34, 76–82.

Bell, R. C. 1960. *Ball and Table Games from Many Civilizations*. London.

Birley, A. 1979. *The People of Roman Britain*. London.

Bishop, M. C., and J. C. Coulston. 2006. *Roman Military Equipment from the Punic Wars to the Fall of Rome*, 2nd ed. Oxford.

Breeze, D. J. 1997. 'The Regiments Stationed at Maryport and Their Commanders'. In *Roman Maryport and Its Setting*. Edited by R. J. A. Wilson, Maryport, pages 67–89.

Brown, A. G., and I. M. Meadows. 2000. 'Roman Vineyards in Britain: Finds from the Nene Valley and New Research'. *Antiquity* 74.285: 491–492.

Buckland, P. C. 1978. 'Cereal Production, Storage and Population: A Caveat'. In *The Effect of Man on the Landscape: The Lowland Zone*. Edited by S. Limbrey and J. G. Evans, CBA Res. Rep. 21, London, pages 43–45.

Casey, P. J. 1984. *Roman Coinage in Britain*, 2nd ed. Princes Risborough.

Cool, H. E. M. 2000. 'The Parts Left Over: Material Culture into the Fifth Century'. In *The Late Roman Transition in the North*. Edited by T. Wilmot and P. Wilson, Oxford, pages 47–65.

Cool, H. E. M. 2004. *The Roman Cemetery at Brougham, Cumbria: Excavations 1966–67*. Britannia Monograph Ser. No. 21, London.

Cool, H. E. M. 2006. *Eating and Drinking in Roman Britain*. Cambridge.

Cool, H. E. M. forthcoming. 'Funerary Use'. In *Artefacts in Roman Britain: Their Purpose and Use*. Edited by L. Allason-Jones, Cambridge.

Curle, J. 1911. *Newstead: A Roman Frontier Post and Its People*. Glasgow.

Dark, K. R. 1994. *Civitas to Kingdom: British Political Continuity, 300–800*. Leicester.

Dark, K. R. 2000. *Britain and the End of the Roman Empire*. Stroud.

Esmonde-Cleary, A. S. 1989. *The Ending of Roman Britain*. London.

Gabra-Sanders, T. 2001. 'The Orkney Hood Re-dated and Re-considered'. In *The Roman Textile Industry and Its Influence*. Edited by P. Walton Rogers, L. B. Jørgensen and A. Rast-Eicher, Oxford, pages 98–104.

Henig, M. 1984. *Religion in Roman Britain*. London.

Jackson, R. 1997. 'An Ancient British Medical Kit from Stanway, Essex'. *Lancet* 350: 1471–1473.

Jackson, R., and T. W. Potter. 1996. *Excavations at Stonea, Cambridgeshire, 1980–85*. London.

Jones, C. P. 1987. '*Stigma*: Tattooing and Branding in Graeco-Roman Antiquity'. *Journal of Roman Studies* 77: 139–155.

Jones, M. 1996. *The End of Roman Britain*. Princeton.

Lewis, M. J. T. 1966. *Temples in Roman Britain*. Cambridge.

Manning, W. H. 1964. 'The Plough in Roman Britain'. *Journal of Roman Studies* 65: 54–65.

Mays, S. 1995. 'Killing the Unwanted Child'. *British Archaeology* 2 (March): 8–9.

Millett, M. 1990. *The Romanization of Britain*. Cambridge.

Moore, C. N. 1975. 'A Roman Bronze Candlestick from Branston, Lincolnshire'. *Britannia* 6: 210–212.

Reece, R. 2002. *The Coinage of Roman Britain*. Stroud.

Rees, S. forthcoming. 'Agriculture'. In *Artefacts in Roman Britain: Their Purpose and Use*. Edited by L. Allason-Jones, Cambridge.

Rivet, A. L. F., and C. Smith. 1979. *The Place-Names of Roman Britain*. London.

Roberts, C., and M. Cox. 2003. *Health and Disease in Britain, from Prehistory to the Modern Day*. Stroud.

Robinson, H. R. 1975. *The Armour of Imperial Rome*. London.

Ross, A. 1974. *Pagan Celtic Britain*, Cardinal ed. London.

Salway, P. 1981. *Roman Britain*. Oxford.

Southern, P. 1989. 'The *Numeri* of the Roman Imperial Army'. *Britannia* 20: 81–140.

Thomas, C. 1981. *Christianity in Roman Britain to AD 500*. London.

Thompson, E. A. 1984. *St Germanus of Auxerre and the End of Roman Britain*. Woodbridge.

Tomlin, R. S. O. 1988. 'The Curse Tablets'. In *The Temple of Sulis Minerva at Bath II: The Finds from the Sacred Spring*. Edited by B. Cunliffe, Oxford, pages 59–269.

Tomlin, R. S. O. 1996. 'A Five-Acre Wood in Roman Kent'. In *Interpreting Roman London: Papers in Memory of Hugh Chapman*. Edited by J. Bird, M. Hassall and H. Sheldon, London, pages 209–215.

Tomlin, R. S. O. 1998. 'Roman Manuscripts from Carlisle: The Ink-Written Tablets'. *Britannia* XXIX: 31–84.

Tomlin, R. S. O. 2003a. 'The Girl in Question: A New Text from Roman London'. *Britannia* 34: 41–51.

Tomlin, R. S. O. 2003b. 'Documenting the Roman Army at Carlisle'. In *Documenting the Roman Army*. Edited by J. J. Wilkes, London, pages 175–187.

Tomlin, R. S. O. 2004. 'A Roman Will from North Wales'. *Archaeologia Cambrensis* 150: 143–156.

Toynbee, J. M. C. 1971; repr. 1996. *Death and Burial in the Roman World*. London; Baltimore and London.

Turner, E. G. 1956. 'A Roman Writing Tablet from Somerset'. *Journal of Roman Studies* 6: 115–118.

Wacher, J. 1974. *The Towns of Roman Britain*. London.

White, R. 2007. *Britannia Prima: Britain's Last Roman Province*. Stroud.

Wild, J. P. 1968. 'Clothing in the North-West Provinces of the Roman Empire'. *Bonner Jahrbucher* 168: 166–240.

Willis, S. 2005. 'The Context of Writing and Written Records in Ink: The Archaeology of Samian Inkwells in Roman Britain'. *Archaeological Journal* 162: 96–145.

Wirth, L. 1938. 'Urbanism as a Way of Life'. *American Journal of Sociology* 44 (July): 1–24.

Woodward, A., and P. Leach. 1993. *The Uley Shrines: Excavation of a Ritual Complex on West Hill, Uley, Gloucestershire, 1977–79*. London.

Wright, R. P. 1968. 'Inscriptions'. *Journal of Roman Studies* 58: 206–214.

Zienkiewicz, J. D. 1986. *The Legionary Fortress Baths at Caerleon II: The Finds*. Cardiff.

Abbreviations

CSIR	*Corpus Signorum Imperii Romani*, vol. I (1977), E. J. Phillips; vol. 1.6 (1988), J. N. C. Coulston and E. J. Phillips, Oxford.
ILS	*Inscriptiones Latinae Selectae.* Edited E. Dessau. 3 volumes. (1925–31) Berlin.
RIB	*The Roman Inscriptions of Britain*, R. G. Collingwood and R. P. Wright (1965), Oxford.
Tab. Sul.	*The Temple of Sulis Minerva at Bath II*: *The Finds from the Sacred Spring*, B. Cunliffe (1988), Oxford.
Tab. Vindol.	*The Vindolanda Writing Tablets (Tabulae Vindolandensis)*, vol. I (1983); vol. II (1994); vol. III (2003), A. K. Bowman and J. D. Thomas, London.

Classical Texts

Aetius *Corpus Medicorum Graecorum*. Edited by A. Olivieri (1950), Berlin.

Augustus *Res Gestae Divi Augusti*. Translated by F. Shipley (1966), Loeb.

Caesar *De Bello Gallico*. Translated by H. J. Edwards (1966), Loeb.

Cassius Dio *Roman History*. Translated by B. Foster (1970), Loeb.

Codex Theodosianus http://www.ucl.ac.uk/history/volterra/texts/cthinfo.htm (cited 30 May 2008).

Columella *De Re Rustica*. Translated by H. Boyd Ash (1977), Loeb.

Diodorus Siculus *Library of History*. Translated by C. H. Oldfather (1952–1975), Loeb.

Herodian *Histories*. Translated by C. Whittaker (1969), Loeb.

Hyginus *Hygini Fabulae*. Translated by H. J. Rose (1934), Leiden.

Justinian *Digest*. Translated by A. Watson (1998), University of Pennsylvania Press.

Ovid *Ars Amatoria*. Translated by F. J. Miller (1916), Loeb.

Palladius *On Husbandrie*. Translated by B. Lodge (1873), Early English Text Society.

Plautus *Casina*. Translated by P. Nixon (1916–1938), Loeb.

Plautus *Cistellaria*. Translated by P. Nixon (1916–1938), Loeb.

Pliny the Younger *Letters*. Translated by B. Radice (1971), Penguin.

Pliny *Naturalis Historia*. Translated by H. Rackham (1967), Loeb.

Plutarch *On the Cessation of Oracles*. *Moralia V*. Translated by F. Babbitt (1936), Loeb (also called 'The Obsolescence of Oracles').

Polybius *The Histories*. Translated by W. R. Paton (1922–1927), Loeb.

Seneca *Epistulae Morales*. Translated by J. W. Basore (1928–1932), Loeb.

Strabo *Geography*. Translated by H. L. Jones (1969), Loeb.

Suetonius *Lives of the Caesars*. Translated by R. Graves (1957), Penguin.

Tacitus *Agricola*. Translated by M. Hutton and R. M. Ogilvie (1970), Loeb.

Tacitus *Annals*. Translated by M. Grant (1985), Penguin.

Tacitus *Germania*. Translated by M. Hutton and E. H. Warrington (1970), Loeb.

Tacitus *Histories*. Translated by C. H. Moore (1968), Loeb.

Tertullian *On Female Dress*. Translated by C. Dodgson (1842), A Library of Fathers of the Holy Catholic Church.

Varro *De Re Rustica*. Translated by W. D. Hooper (1967), Loeb.

Vegetius *Epitome of Military Science*. Translated by N. P. Milner (1996, 2nd ed.), Liverpool.

Virgil *Georgics*. Translated by H. Rushton Fairclough (1916), Loeb.

Vita Melania. Translated by E. A. Clark (1984), Edwin Mellen Press.

Vitruvius *On Architecture*. Translated by F. Granger (1962), Loeb.

Zosimus *Historia Nova*. Translated by F. Pachoud (1971).

About the Author

Lindsay Allason-Jones was, until 2008, Director of Archaeological Museums for Newcastle University before becoming the director of the Centre for Interdisciplinary Artefact Studies at Newcastle University where she is also Reader in Roman Material Culture. She has published many books and papers on the archaeology of the Roman Empire, particularly on artefacts and issues relating to women in the provinces. She is involved in the governance of many of the museums on Hadrian's Wall and is also a member of a number of international, national and regional bodies concerned with the dissemination of archaeological knowledge to the public.

Index